SENSE & SENSIBILITY

Honoring God With My Life

An Expositional Study of Titus 2:3-5

Miriam Nadler

TABLE OF CONTENTS

FOREWORD

Shalom,

"For I am confident of this very thing, that He who began a good work in you will perfect it until the day of Messiah Yeshua*" (Philippians 1:6). This is one of my favorite verses as I realize daily that it is the Lord who will accomplish in me and through me what He desires. As this material that I have taught for a number of years is now in book form, I see it as one more evidence that through weakness His power is perfected.

I want to thank my husband Sam. His passion for the Word of God and gift of teaching the Word have been a constant inspiration to me. Sam's counsel and mentoring me to study for myself and see what the text says gave me the confidence to prepare and teach this material.

I am especially thankful for my friend, Natalia Fomin. She not only has a passionate heart to see women discipled but a deep love for the Word of God.

Natalia was a continual source of encouragement as we worked together to see this project completed. Her belief in the value of the material gave me the desire to keep writing. Her friendship is truly a gift from the Lord and a confirmation of how God can use us to make a difference for eternity as we seek to honor the Lord with our lives. Natalia is truly a woman of excellence!

Thank you, Nanci Erkert for all your work on editing the manuscript in the midst of your busy schedule as you minister around the world.

I am also thankful for the wonderful women at Hope of Israel Congregation for their prayers and encouragement as I taught this material.

This book is written not only for your personal study but for one on one mentoring or small group study. The thought questions and reflections at the end of each chapter will be helpful to lead interactive discussions.

This book is written from a Messianic Jewish frame of reference with the goal of pointing to Yeshua the Messiah whom we seek to serve.

The prayer of my heart is that this book will encourage you to honor the Lord with your life and deepen your walk in Him!

In His Grace,

Miriam Nadler

* Yeshua is the Jewish way to say Jesus.

FROM THE AUTHOR

During my college years as a very young believer, I was discipled by Arnold Fruchtenbaum, who is a Jewish believer in Jesus and now leads Ariel Ministries. For some reason, Arnold saw in me ministry potential, even though I was basically immature and untaught in the Scriptures. As he discipled me in aspects of the faith, like believing God to provide for my school bill as I worked my way through college, he also gave me an understanding and love for the Jewish people. He encouraged me to write my papers for English and History on various aspects of Jewish life, especially the Holocaust. I became involved in Arnold's prayer group for Israel, and the Lord put a burden on my heart to reach out to Jewish people.

I spent four summers ministering in Brooklyn, New York with Hilda Koser, who was one of the great Jewish missionaries for Messiah. As I worked alongside her during the summer Bible school outreaches in Coney Island, NY, Miss Koser taught me how to minister to children.

The Lord provided another mentor in my life: Ruth Wardell. She was a Gentile believer in Messiah who made a profound impact for the Lord among Jewish young people.

As a counselor at Camp Sar Shalom for Jewish teenagers, I watched Ruth interact with them. With her example and encouragement and by God's grace, I was able to have a positive impact on the lives of a number of young women as a camp counselor and Bible teacher.

After graduating from Cedarville University with my degree in teaching, I knew that the Lord was calling me into Jewish ministry. I taught for a short time in public school to pay off my college bills then moved to New York City to work with *Chosen People Ministries* (then the American Board of Missions to the Jews). I moved to New York City with great joy and anticipation because I knew that the Lord was leading me.

During my first six months in the city, I studied under Moishe Rosen, who later started *Jews for Jesus*. I immersed myself in Jewish culture, learning the Hebrew language and Israeli music. I began a small women's Bible study. We met every Friday night on the Upper West Side in the building that Chosen People Ministries then owned. I would often cook a meal, where about a dozen ladies would gather to study and be discipled. This was my first experience of teaching a women's Bible study, and I was certainly a novice. I was only 21 years old, and some of the women were twice my age.

After three years of ministry in New York City, I had the privilege of moving to Israel, where I studied at Hebrew University in Jerusalem for a year and took some post graduate courses. I also studied Hebrew at an *ulpan*, which is an intensive language school. But that year in Israel turned out to be not merely a time to study but a time to minister. Through one on one friendships and a coffee house outreach in Jerusalem that I helped to start, I had various opportunities to share my faith. After my year of study and outreach in Israel, I moved back to New York City.

Later the Lord led me to move to California to help start *Jews for Jesus*. When we began a music team called *The Liberated Wailing Wall*, I met a new believer named Sam Nadler. In chapter two I will tell the story of how we met. The Lord definitely brought us together in love and in ministry.

For the first few years of our married lives we were on the road, crisscrossing the USA doing concerts for both evangelistic outreach and to raise support. Eventually our touring days ended, and Sam and I moved to New York City. We began our outreach work there by opening the New York branch of *Jews for Jesus*. I started discipling women one on one and in small groups.

In 1979, God called Sam to provide leadership for *Chosen People Ministries* (CPM), which he did until 1996. As CPM's NYC Director, Sam first mobilized the staff to engage in team-oriented outreach that was bold, creative, and culturally relevant. This served to enhance the ministry's local profile and evangelistic productivity.

Along with raising our two sons, Josh and Matt, I served alongside of Sam who had become Northeast Regional Director for CPM. Convinced that the Great Commission meant evangelism that produced discipled believers, we began personally planting as well as supervising the planting of several Messianic congregations in the Northeast US. As God's blessing on our ministry became evident, Sam was asked to lead the worldwide organization in 1989.

As President of CPM, Sam brought new strategic intent to the global work. With the Great Commission as his objective, Sam launched the century-old Jewish ministry in a new strategic direction: the planting of Messianic congregations among the Jewish people. When Sam and I began *Word of Messiah Ministries* in 1997, we wanted to concentrate on helping to build up congregations through practical discipleship materials.

Early on in our new ministry, Sam was asked to return to Berlin, Germany to help the congregational planters that he had encouraged in the past. They wanted him to teach men and women separately to give practical wisdom from the Scriptures to be godly men and women. As a result of that invitation, Sam did an in-depth study of Titus 2:3-5. He found it to be so meaningful that he taught it to me and encouraged me to 'make it my own' with my own study and application.

These past 8 years, I have done just that. I have taught the material contained in this book in Messianic congregations here in the States, in Eastern Europe and in Israel. Each time I see the positive effect the Word of God has as it is understood and applied. This teaching is invaluable for women of all ages in understanding how to mature and live for the Lord today.

Whether you are older or younger, single or married - wherever you are in your life's journey as a believer, I pray that this expositional study of Titus 2:3-5 will be helpful to you.

For Messiah's Glory,

Miriam Nadler

*A Woman of Excellence opens
her mouth in wisdom, and
the teaching of kindness
is on her tongue.*

Proverbs 31:26

אֵשֶׁת־חַיִל

Chapter 1

YOUR DIVINE CALLING

QUALIFIED TO TEACH

*Older woman likewise are to be reverent in their behavior,
not malicious gossips, nor enslaved to much wine, teaching
what is good, that they may encourage the young women to
love their husbands, to love their children, to be sensible, pure,
workers at home, kind, being subject to their own husbands,
that the word of God may not be dishonored.*
Titus 2:3-5

Do you ever feel as if the whole world has gone crazy? Or maybe you feel like you are going to jump out of your skin during "that time of the month." Throughout my married years, especially when my two sons were young, there were numerous times when I thought I was going out of my mind. My PMS symptoms would be raging, and I would find it difficult to keep my emotions in check. I also suffered from low self-esteem which seems to be a plague that affects many women. I earnestly wanted to be a godly wife and mother. After all, God had called us into full time ministry.

Therefore, I needed to be a role model and set an example for other women. I believe that this portion in Titus can teach us how to be the women that God wants us to be. We are all striving to be women who honor God, whether we are older, younger, single, married, divorced or remarried. We need to realize that we cannot live up to the qualities that are given in Titus 2:3-5 and live out our biblical mandate unless we acknowledge day-by-day our total dependence on the Lord.

God knows our needs because He created us with these needs. It is important for us to understand from the outset that our career, our home, our wealth (or lack of it), our husband, or our children can never meet our needs. We are created as the sheep of His hand, to be dependent on Him alone, and He wants us to acknowledge our total dependence on Him. The Lord is our Shepherd. He will meet all our needs. Therefore, we must yield our hearts to Him even as we begin this study together.

As we seek to become a woman after God's own heart, we will be studying word by word Titus 2:3-5. As we look deeply into the Word of God, we will study the original words in Greek and Hebrew to help us understand both the context and the meaning. We will be transformed by applying these truths and living our lives accordingly. It might seem challenging at first, but it will be greatly rewarding.

I am convinced that what God has to say in this portion is not merely relevant and vital but necessary if our lives are to bring honor and glory to the Lord.

INTRODUCTION TO THE BOOK OF TITUS

This letter was written by Paul to Titus, his child in the faith. Titus was faced with the task of establishing order in the congregations at Crete (Titus 1:5). The letter was written to help Titus understand how to do it.

Part of the "setting in order" and establishing healthy congregations is related to putting people in their right minds or what I call *Sense and Sensibilities*. In chapter two of Titus, the Greek word for *sensible* is repeated five times.

> Titus 2:2, 4-6, 12—Older men are to be temperate, dignified, *sensible*, sound in faith, in love, in perseverance. 4. That they may *encourage* the young women to love their husbands, to love their children, 5. To be *sensible*, pure, workers at home, kind, being subject to their own husbands, that the word of God may not be dishonored. 6. Likewise urge the young men to be *sensible*; 12. Instructing us to deny ungodliness and worldly desires and to live *sensibly*, righteously and godly in the present age.

To describe the older men (v. 2), the young women (v. 5), the young men (v. 6), and all of us who want to live godly lives (v. 12), a form of the Greek word *sophron* is used which means to be of sound mind, temperate, or have sound judgment. The verb form, *sophronizo* (Titus 2:4) means to recall one to her senses, to admonish, and to train one to be of right mind. In the context of the older men, it is *sensible*. In the context of women, it is used two times and translated *encourage* and *sensible*. In the context of young men it is also *sensible*. In truth, all people are to live *sensibly*.

I think we get the point that this chapter in Titus (and our study) has the goal of putting us into our right minds or encouraging sound judgment. This is the overarching theme of our study of Titus 2:3-5.

Who Is To Be Taught?

The Scriptures tell us that older women are to teach younger women. But when the text says "younger women", it does not refer only to physical age. In the original language, it also reflects the idea of newness. Actually, there are three areas for consideration.

First, at what age is it appropriate for an older woman to teach a younger woman? Physical age has to do with a young woman reaching puberty.

In our society, it seems to be getting younger each year. Let me put it this way: you have a young daughter, and until now she could care less about what she wears to school, but all of a sudden she begins to be very concerned about how she dresses and what others think of her.

At this point, your daughter needs to be encouraged and trained in the issues of sense and sensibility.

This portion of Titus 2:3-5 will help put her in her right mind about who she is as a young woman.

Secondly, it also has to do with spiritual age. As we read in Colossians 3:10 "and have put on the *new* self who is being renewed to a true knowledge according to the image of the One who created him."

A new believer in Messiah needs to reorient her life and her understanding of the issues that are taught in Titus so that she has a biblical perspective. She needs to be discipled and mature in her faith in order to honor God.

Some women have been believers for many years but are still spiritually immature, because they have never been discipled in the areas that we will discuss.

The third area of being a *young* woman has to do with starting over. This applies to a woman who has had her life shipwrecked by a traumatic experience that has decimated her faith.

Perhaps this woman has gone through a terrible divorce, the death of a child, or a health issue in which she was not able to trust the Lord. She feels that her faith is no longer relevant to her life. This woman needs to be lovingly restored to the Lord.

Who Can Teach?

Now that we have taken a look at who is to be taught, it's time to understand who can teach. The Scriptures tell us that the older women are to be teachers.

This idea of older women is not so much about physical age as maturity, as seen in her behavior as a believer.

Let us look at Titus 2:2, where Paul gives a list of the qualities regarding older men. "Older men are to be temperate, dignified, sensible, sound in faith, in love, in perseverance."

Paul then goes on to explain that older women likewise, or in the same way, are to exemplify certain qualities.

The four qualities that older women are to possess are found in Titus 2:3

- ❧ REVERENT IN THEIR BEHAVIOR
- ❧ NOT MALICIOUS GOSSIPS
- ❧ NOR ENSLAVED TO MUCH WINE
- ❧ TEACHING WHAT IS GOOD

REVERENT IN THEIR BEHAVIOR

What does *reverent in thier behavior* mean? It carries the idea of holy living. The prophet Isaiah gives us a glimpse of what this reverent behavior looks like as he describes the throne room of the Most High God.

> Isaiah 6:1-3—In the year of King Uzziah's death, I saw the Lord sitting on a throne, lofty and exalted, with the train of His robe filling the temple. Seraphim stood above Him, each having six wings; with two he covered his face, and with two he covered his feet, and with two he flew. And one called out to another and said, "Holy, Holy, Holy, is the LORD of hosts, the whole earth is full of His glory.

What were the Seraphim doing in heaven? How did their behavior reflect their reverence for God?

It says in verse 2 that with two wings they covered their faces as a sign of awe, with two wings they covered their feet as a sign of modesty, and with two wings they flew, always ready to serve, as they proclaimed, "Holy, Holy, Holy."

The word "holy" in the Hebrew is *kadosh*, which means sacred, holy, or set apart.

We can learn much from these angelic beings. They were created to bring honor and glory to the only One who is worthy. And this is also why God created you and me: to enjoy an intimate relationship that would glorify Him.

As an older woman who is a child of God, that's what I want my life to be all about. I desire to bring honor and glory to the Lord by my behavior and my walk in Him. I want to be reverent, modest, and ready to serve Him.

These Seraphim are not bringing attention to themselves but to the Lord of Hosts, who is the only One worthy of honor.

Not malicious gossips

The next quality to be found in older women is "not malicious gossips." In reading *The Measure of a Woman* by Gene and Elaine Getz, I found the way that they described and compared the qualifications for male and female leaders to be both helpful and interesting.

For men, it says in 1 Timothy 3:2 "that men are to be above reproach and the husband of one wife."

It is repeated in Titus 1:6 that men are "to be blameless and the husband of one wife." The qualifications that are reiterated for female leaders in 1 Timothy 3:11 says that "women are to be worthy of respect and not malicious talkers" and in Titus 2:3, we read that women are to be "reverent in the way they live and not malicious gossips."

Gene Getz explains:

> What was Paul saying about the differences between men and women and how these variations can affect our reputations? Clearly, a man's major temptation and weakness is sexual (to be immoral). Stated positively, moral purity does more to build a man's reputation than do all the qualities that follow on Paul's list. On the other hand, women's major temptation and weakness is verbal (to communicate in ways that are destructive). Stated positively, a woman who controls her tongue and is a peacemaker does more to build her reputation than having all the other qualities Paul listed. This, of course, does not mean that both men and women are not tempted in both areas. What it does mean, however, is that based on gender, these are areas of vulnerability and weakness that can also become areas of strength and thus build men's and women's reputations.

In the phrase "malicious gossips," the Greek word for malicious gossip is *diabolos* which means slanderous or accusing falsely. It's the same word that is used for the devil. We must not underestimate how offensive gossip is to the Lord. It is through our speech that we grieve the Holy Spirit.

> Ephesians 4:29-32—Let no unwholesome word proceed from your mouth, but only such a word as is good for edification according to the need of the moment, that it may give grace to those who hear. And do not grieve the Holy Spirit of God, by whom you were sealed for the day of redemption. Let all bitterness and wrath and anger and clamor and slander be put away from you, along with all malice. And be kind to one another, tender-hearted, forgiving each other, just as God in Messiah also has forgiven you.

When we slander, accuse falsely, or defame someone else, we are buying into Satan's program.

The enemy of our souls is the father of lies. John 8:44 says, "He (Satan) was a murderer from the beginning, and does not stand in the truth, because there is no truth in him. Whenever he speaks a lie, he speaks from his own nature; for he is a liar, and the father of lies."

In contrast, we serve a God who cannot lie. As we read in Titus 1:2, "In the hope of eternal life, which God, who cannot lie, promised long ages ago."

There is no condemnation

Satan is not only the father of lies, he is also the accuser of the brethren. Revelation 12:10 says, "And I heard a loud voice in heaven, saying, 'Now the salvation, and the power, and the kingdom of our God and the authority of His Messiah have come, for the accuser of our brethren has been thrown down, who accuses them before our God day and night.'"

Praise God this scene from heaven shows that Satan has been defeated! But the devil is still accusing you and me today. Therefore, it is important to know the difference between feeling accused and condemned for our actions, (which is the specialty of the evil one), and feeling convicted by the Holy Spirit. Feeling condemned leads to despair, self-hatred, and guilt. In contrast, conviction leads to confession and forgiveness. For example, if I lie to someone, Satan will start to accuse me. "Look! You lied, yet you call yourself a believer? You're just a big, fat, no good liar!"

In contrast, the Holy Spirit convicts me: "Miriam, you told a lie, so you need to confess it to God and have the intimacy of your relationship restored."

As our intimacy with the Lord is restored, we confirm the truth of God's Word that "There is therefore now no condemnation for those who are in Messiah Yeshua" (Romans 8:1).

MASTER TRUTH-TWISTER

The devil is also a twister of the truth. This plays into the idea of malicious gossiping, as truth can be misconstrued and twisted to hurt and to harm. When Messiah was tempted by the devil in the wilderness, the devil used truths from Scripture and twisted them to suit his purpose. Satan wanted to discredit Messiah and terminate His earthly ministry. He failed because Yeshua was able to draw on truth from the Word of God to refute the evil intentions of Satan (Luke 4:1-13).

In contrast to Yeshua, who withstood the test of Satan, Eve was deceived by that crafty serpent as he twisted the words of God. In order to understand more fully this idea of how we as women can misuse our tongues, we need to go back to Genesis. God is instructing Adam regarding his duties and the one tree that he is not to eat from:

> Genesis 2:16-17—And the Lord God commanded the man, saying, "From any tree of the garden you may eat freely; but from the tree of the knowledge of good and evil you shall not eat, for in the day that you eat from it you shall surely die."

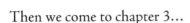

Then we come to chapter 3...

> Genesis 3:1-5—Now the serpent was more crafty than any beast of the field which the LORD God had made. And he said to the woman, "Indeed, has God said, You shall not eat from any tree of the garden?" And the woman said to the serpent, "From the fruit of the trees of the garden we may eat; but from the fruit of the tree which is in the middle of the garden, God has said, 'You shall not eat from it or *touch it*, lest you die.' And the serpent said to the woman, "You surely shall not die! For God knows that in the day you eat from it your eyes will be opened, and you will be like God, knowing good and evil."

Notice that the devil is slandering God by implying that He is trying to prevent Eve from acquiring godlike knowledge and thus becoming like Him (Genesis 3:5). He also twists the truth. Eve opened herself up to his truth-twisting because she was not accurate when describing the commands given to her by God. She added to God's Word. As we read in verse 3... "but from the fruit of the tree which is in the middle of the garden, God has said, You shall not eat from it or *touch it*, lest you die." God never said anything to Adam about *not touching* the tree. By adding to the Word of God, Eve opened herself up to the lies of Satan. Do you realize the damage that twisting God's truth can have on you and on those whose lives you influence?

When we gossip, we need to remember that we are playing into the schemes of the enemy of our souls. How many congregations have been split or lives devastated because of the malicious gossip of resentful women? This brings us to another aspect that we need to consider regarding our speech.

Keeping Confidences

If an older woman is not to be a malicious gossip, the implication is that she will keep what she hears confidential. In other words, you can be assured that what you share with her will remain private. You must be able to trust the older woman who disciples you.

I think that many times we do not understand what constitutes gossip. Slandering or talking about someone who is not there is gossiping, even if it is done under the guise of "needing prayer." "Pray for Esther. She is having problems with that no good husband of hers who I heard was caught sleeping with his secretary...but I won't mention her name." Not only does gossip slander people who are not present, it also defiles those who give ear to gossip.

We women like to be kept in the loop, but we have to be careful when we counsel not to fall into the sin of gossiping. I had to learn these concepts in the midst of ministry. As I matured and ministered, I found that many times women would come to me for counseling, expecting their needs to be kept confidential. I learned how important it was to be trustworthy in this area.

I also discovered that the very best thing that a counselor can do for anyone who comes to her for advice is to point her to the Wonderful Counselor (Isaiah 9:6). I encourage those who come to me to put their situations on the Lord and not to rely solely on people. The Scriptures exhort us, "Casting all your anxiety on Him for He cares for you" (1 Peter 5:7).

In her book, *A Woman's High Calling*, Elizabeth George gives a helpful list to those who would want to avoid gossip. Many of us have been in situations where we wanted to be kind and minister to the gossiper, but after listening and giving ear to the gossip, we felt remorse, wishing it had never happened. I have to include Elizabeth's list because it is practical and helpful:

- Leave the scene: Joseph in the Old Testament shows us vividly how to flee from sin (Genesis 39:12)! So flee! Leave the room! Get out! ASAP! Excuse yourself. Go get a breath of fresh air…. and while you are out of earshot, shoot a prayer to God. Ask Him for His wisdom concerning the best way to handle the particular situation.

- Declare your discomfort: Speak up. Say something like, "I'm sorry. Maybe it's me, but I'm not comfortable with this conversation. Could we please change the subject?"

- Guard your facial expressions. Unfortunately, we can "gossip" or plant seeds of doubt or smear someone's reputation without a word. How? By the use of our face and eyes. Who hasn't wondered when someone else rolled her eyes or shook her head, or raised her eyebrows in a knowing manner or grimaced at the mention of another's name? Be sure that you don't communicate negatively about people in these telltale ways.

- Another type of phrase that instantly raises my guard is any variation on "Don't tell anyone, but…" At that point, I raise both hands and interrupt with, "Well, please don't tell me!"

Before we move to the third, let us quickly review the first two qualities that an older woman must seek to attain.

The first area of growth for a teaching woman is her walk in the Lord. She seeks to bring glory to the Lord with her life. The second area is her speech, as she seeks to keep all that she says under control. As Paul reiterates, "Let no unwholesome word proceed from your mouth, but only such a word as is good for edification according to the need of the moment, that it may give grace to those who hear" (Ephesians 5:29).

NOT ENSLAVED TO MUCH WINE

Now let's examine the third desirable quality for older women who teach: "nor enslaved to much wine." When it says "don't be enslaved" it conveys the idea of not being under bondage or addicted to wine. Instead of being under the influence of wine, the mature woman is to let her life be controlled by the Holy Spirit.

> Ephesians 5:15-20—Therefore be careful how you walk, not as unwise men, but as wise, making the most of your time, because the days are evil. So then do not be foolish, but understand what the will of the Lord is. And do not get drunk with wine, for that is dissipation, but be filled with the Spirit, speaking to one another in psalms and hymns and spiritual songs, singing and making melody with your heart to the Lord; always giving thanks for all things in the name of our Lord Yeshua the Messiah to God, even the Father.

Of course allowing the Holy Spirit to control us is the only way to break any addictive habit that we might have, whether it be an addiction to wine, to exercise, to food, to shopping, to being a people pleaser, or to anything else.

A mature woman's life is under the control of the Holy Spirit with a balanced life style.

TEACHING WHAT IS GOOD

Being the verbal gender is both a great strength and a great weakness. We need to be not just talkers but teachers, and teachers of what is good. We need to know what is worthwhile to speak about, what is worthless, and what will get us into trouble.

The final area for the older woman is teaching what is good. A woman who does this knows what is excellent, worthwhile, or of value. Some of you are excellent shoppers. My sister has a knack for finding clothes of good quality when they are marked down as much as 75%. I love it when she goes shopping with me because I don't have the patience or the eye to tell what is good and what isn't. But my sister can say, "Try this dress on, Miriam, it will look great on you." Even though I may have my doubts, because I know I can trust her, I try on the dress. Wonder of wonders, it looks great and is a bargain to boot!

Likewise, the wise teacher needs to understand what is worth being taught. Paul's exhortation to the congregation at Philippi will give us insight as to how this works.

> Philippians 4:6-9—Be anxious for nothing, but in everything by prayer and supplication with thanksgiving let your requests be made known to God. And the peace of God, which surpasses all comprehension, shall guard your hearts and your minds in Messiah Yeshua. Finally, brethren, whatever is true, whatever is honorable,

whatever is right, whatever is pure, whatever is lovely, whatever is of good repute, if there is any excellence and if anything worthy of praise, let your mind dwell on these things. The things you have learned and received and heard and seen in me, practice these things; and the God of peace shall be with you.

Many of us are familiar with these verses which tell us not to worry about anything but to throw our burdens on the Lord through prayer with thanksgiving. As we lift our requests to the Lord, His shalom - His peace - will surround our hearts and minds with His protection. The Hebrew word for guard or protect is *shomer*. It is found in a number of Scriptures like Psalm 121:4, "Behold, He who keeps Israel will neither slumber nor sleep." Unlike those of us who have insomnia issues, God never slumbers or sleeps; He is always keeping Israel and you. The word "keep" is the word *shomer*, which also means "guard." Think of your heart and mind as having God's watchmen around them, protecting you and giving you His shalom as a result.

I want to focus on verse 8 for a moment because understanding what this verse says for my own life has helped me to realize what it means to have the peace of God surround both my emotions and my thought life. It has also helped me to understand what I should teach.

Philippians 4:8 –Finally, brethren, whatever is true, whatever is honorable, whatever is right, whatever is pure, whatever is lovely, whatever is of good repute, if there is any excellence and if anything worthy of praise, let your mind dwell on these things.

Here Paul lists a number of qualities. Let's begin by examining the first one: "Whatever is true." Whatever is true… hmmm, let's see. As I watch the news this morning, I know that it's true that, "Hurricane Katrina has done untold damage to the Gulf Coast." And it's true that I received a call from my sister saying that my mother had been admitted to the hospital.

Now, how can thinking about these true things bring me to God's peace? Or take the last aspect in the list, "whatever is worthy of praise." Those in the Hollywood lifestyle would tell me that many people are "worthy of praise." There are Oscars, Golden Globes, and Life Time Achievement Awards to honor them, as well as the Nobel Peace Prizes that are given to those who are deemed worthy of praise and honor in other fields. But how is this helpful to me in light of Philippians 4:8? Here is a news flash: It doesn't work that way! What our secular society deems worthy of praise, noble, or of good report is not even close to what the Scriptures teach us.

When Paul says "whatever is true," he is referring to the One who is Himself Truth. The Greek word that is used for "true" in Philippians 4:8 is the same word found in John 14:6 when Messiah says, "I am the way, and the truth, and the life."

We have already mentioned Titus 1:2, which reminds us that we have a God who cannot lie. Looking at the list in Philippians our minds are to dwell upon: whatever is true, honorable, right, pure, lovely, of good reputation, excellent, and worthy of praise.

This list reflects the character of God and His promises to us. This provides the basis for teaching what is good and should be the content of our teaching.

When I think of the women who have mentored me and had a profound influence in my life, one in particular stands out. I mentioned Ruth Wardell in my introduction. I met her in New York when I was first starting out in ministry over thirty-seven years ago. As an effective Gentile missionary to the Jewish people, she was a role model for me. All of these years later, when I compare her life to the four qualifications in Titus 2:3, I see that she indeed was an "older woman" to me.

Let me go down the checklist:

Was Ruth reverent in her behavior? Yes. Her life was all about honoring the Lord. She lived and ministered in Long Island, New York and although she was not married, she led many Jews and Gentiles to the Lord. Her spiritual children and her relationship with the Lord gave her a fulfilling life.

Was Ruth a gossiper? No, quite the opposite. I remember her being a source of encouragement to me and to many others while able to keep the confidences that were given her.

Was Ruth addicted to much wine? No. Her life was about pleasing the Lord. She kept herself as healthy as she could and was a role model to me in her balanced life style.

Was Ruth teaching what is good? A resounding "yes" on this one. The thing I remember most about Ruth is her positive attitude and enthusiasm for God's Word.

Her positive outlook on life did not come from a problem free ministry or from looking at life through "rose colored glasses" but rather because she knew the secret to having her heart and mind guarded by the shalom of God. She was able to teach that which is true, honorable, right, pure, lovely, of good reputation, excellent, and worthy of praise. Her teaching was based on the character of God and His promises.

Thirty-eight years later, I say, "Thank you, Ruth, for letting the light of Messiah shine brightly through you." Thank you for being an older woman of God.

I trust that these four qualities will challenge all of us. Even if you are a "younger woman" in your spiritual growth, the Lord desires for you to mature and to become an older woman who can disciple and mentor those younger women He will place in your life.

How To Teach

Now that we have discussed the qualifications of the teacher, let's consider how she is to teach the younger women, as reflected in the phrase: "that they may encourage the young women" (Titus 2:4).

We mentioned the Greek word "encourage" in the beginning of this chapter. I think it needs to be repeated because it is related to the theme of our study.

The word "encourage" is *sophronizo*, (Titus 2:4) which means to recall one to her senses or admonish. In other words, the teaching that older women pass on to younger women should put them in their right mind or give them sound judgment.

Another aspect of this word was made clear to me several years ago when I was teaching this study to a wonderful group of women in Israel. One of the ladies shared excitedly that this word "encourage" in her Hebrew Bible is *yashar*, the verb form "to make straight." If you ask for directions in Israel and they tell you to go *yashar*, it means to go straight. This Israeli woman then quoted, "trust in the LORD with all your heart, and do not lean on your own understanding. In all your ways acknowledge Him, And He will make your paths *straight*" [using the same Hebrew word, *yashar*] (Proverbs 3:5-6).

For this woman, Titus 2:4 said, "Straighten out the thinking." That is exactly what we need to do. As younger women are put in their right minds concerning the seven qualities that we see in Titus 2:3-5, the Lord will straighten out their thinking, giving them a biblical perspective on their lives.

Why Do We Teach?

Before we close this chapter, we need to ask WHY? Why should we bother to teach anything at all? Look at the end of verse 5 for the answer, "that the Word of God may not be dishonored."

The transliteration of the Greek word *blasphemeo* is "dishonor," from which we derive the word *blaspheme*. What does this mean? Blaspheme means to slander, hence to speak lightly or profanely of sacred things. In Romans 1:21, Paul gives us an indication of what happens when men do not honor God.

He says, "For even though they knew God, they did not honor Him as God, or give thanks; but they became futile in their speculations, and their foolish heart was darkened."

I would like to look briefly at the Hebrew word for "honor," which is *kavod*: to be heavy or weighty. This will date myself, but I remember when it was cool to say, "Wow! That's heavy," when someone had just said something profound or had given some awesome news. When our lives blaspheme or dishonor the Word of God, we show that we take lightly the Lord and His Word.

On the other hand, when our lives honor the Word of God, we give Him His due weight of glory, which is our reasonable service. The primary meaning of honor is to give the Lord preeminence or first place. He alone is worthy. We give God His due weight of glory.

Paul says that if we do not encourage (put in their right minds) the younger women in these seven areas, then the Word of God will be dishonored, disgraced, shamed, and disparaged in our lives, in our homes, and in our respective congregations.

This teaching is not optional. It is mandatory if we are to mature as women of God. As we study together, we need to keep in mind that our goal for understanding these seven areas of discipleship is to bring honor to the Lord.

Questions for reflection and discussion

1. Are you a younger woman? An older woman? Both? Think of where you are in these areas and how you want to grow as a result of this study.

2. Why does God want us to be in our right minds or have sound judgment?

3. Is the Word of God being dishonored in your life? In your home? In your congregation?

4. What are some examples of how the Word of God is dishonored or taken lightly?

5. Think of women who have discipled you. Perhaps you could send them a note of appreciation. Pray that the Lord would mature you to be an older woman who can teach.

6. If you had your choice and could pick any woman of the Bible, who would you want to be your mentor or older woman?

The heart of her husband trusts in her,
and he will have no lack of gain.
She does him good and not evil
all the days of her life.

Proverbs 31:11-12

Chapter 2

WHO NEEDS MARRIAGE?

WHY CAN'T I JUST LIVE WITH THE GUY?

Is having a husband out of vogue in today's society? In the book *What Our Mothers Didn't Tell Us* or *Why Happiness Eludes the Modern Woman*, Danielle Crittenden writes:

> A twenty year old Ivy League student said that she was planning to have children outside of marriage because she feared a husband might "threaten her individuality."

This insightful author goes on to say:

> Virtually every young woman I interviewed put her job aspirations ahead of any hopes for marriage or children (even if she claimed to want those things eventually). Each one of them worried that a serious attachment to a man, or worse, to children, might compromise her sense of who she was. Few of the women interviewed had read Betty Friedan's *The Feminine Mystique* or other feminist classics and only a handful had joined campus women's groups. It didn't matter. Their generation had provided the laboratory mice for the social experiments of the past twenty-five years.

They had grown up with working mothers, day care, and no-fault divorce. Their primary school textbooks were illustrated with little girls flying planes and little boys mopping floors. They took coed classes in shop and metalworking instead of home economics. They would participate in frank discussions about birth control and sexuality with grade-school teachers. Their developing intellects had been bombarded by feminist cultural messages. The students I interviewed had neither adopted nor rejected feminism. Rather, it had seeped into their minds like intravenous saline into the arm of an unconscious patient. They were feminists without knowing it.

Being A Husband-Lover

Ladies, wouldn't you agree that we need to reevaluate our thinking regarding marriage and having a husband? As a result of this need, in this chapter we will study the quality of being a husband-lover.

"When Paul wrote his letter to Titus, he recorded the most comprehensive list of qualities for measuring a woman's character and true beauty that we can find any place in the New Testament" (Gene Getz, *The Measure of a Woman*).

> Titus 2:3-5—Older women likewise are to be reverent in their behavior, not malicious gossips, nor enslaved to much wine, teaching what is good, so that they may encourage the young women *to love (their) husbands*, to love (their) children, to be sensible, pure, workers at home, kind, being subject to their own husbands, so that the word of God will not be dishonored.

Older women are to teach younger women. The first subject that is brought to our attention is the phrase: "to love (their) husbands."

In the original language the possessive pronoun is not used, and the word that is used is the compound Greek word *philandros*. *Phileo* means love and *andros* means man or husband, so when we translate it, literally, it would be "[a women] loving men" or a "husband-lover." Since the final issue in this list of seven qualities for young women is "being subject to their own husbands," I believe that it makes sense for us to understand that this phrase is not about loving one husband in particular, but about loving the idea of having a husband in general.

This is a mandate for older women to teach younger women if they are to understand God's perspective on marriage.

Well, you may ask, since this is all Greek to me, why is it important? What's so important about not having the pronoun in the original text, which the translators added for readability?

My husband Sam was the first to teach me this grammatical truth. As he studied this section systematically, it became clear to him that since the pronoun is not there in the phrase, "husband lovers," it becomes a general principle for all women, whether married or not.

Let's examine a few more Greek words. The three words for love will be familiar to some of you. They are: *agape* referring to God's love, *phileo* referring to brotherly love, and *eros* referring to erotic love. Many of us may recognize this word *phileo*, because it is where we get our English word Philadelphia, the city of brotherly love.

According to *The Bible Dictionary* by Tyndale, *phileo* love is the alternative word for *agapao* or *agape* love.

There is considerable overlapping of usage between the two words. *Phileo* is more naturally used to express intimate affection, as in the following Scriptures.

John 11:3 – The sisters therefore sent to Him, saying, "Lord, behold, he whom You love (*phileo*) is sick.

John 11:36 – And so the Jews were saying, Behold how He loved (*phileo*) him!

Revelation 3:19 – Those whom I love, (*phileo*) I reprove and discipline; be zealous therefore, and repent.

Often the word *phileo* is understood to designate a unilateral (one-sided) love that is not dependent on the object or person being loved to return the same affection. In other words, *phileo* love is very independent. It is an unconditional love, much as the *agape* love that God has for his children. He loved us when we did not love Him (Romans 5:8).

Back To Genesis

We need to teach the Biblical concept of marriage based on God's perspective on the matter. Older women are to teach younger women to be "husband-lovers," that is, to understand God's concept of marriage and relationships leading up to marriage and to respect what God values. As I teach this passage, again and again I see the desperate need for believing women to comprehend and apply this teaching.

Let's get back to basics. What is marriage and who initiated it? In Genesis we read:

Genesis 2:22-24 —And the LORD God fashioned into a woman the rib which He had taken from the man, and brought her to the man. And the man said, this is now bone of my bones, and flesh of my flesh; she shall be called Woman, because she was taken out of Man. For this cause a man shall leave his father and his mother, and shall cleave to his wife; and they shall become one flesh.

It was God's idea! The Lord said in Genesis 2:18, "It is not good for the man to be alone; I will make him a helper suitable for him."

Marriage - More Than Meets The Eye

God saw the big picture and knew that it was not a good thing for man to be void of an intimate human relationship. Because God is concerned with relationships, He created man to be in relationship with Him and designed marriage specifically to picture certain aspects of His love and His relationship with Israel and the body of believers. God sees marriage as a type (picture or shadow) of His covenant relationship with both Israel and the body of believers in Messiah. The prophet Hosea pictures the Lord's love for Israel through the marriage of Hosea to Gomer.

Messiah's love for the body of Messiah is expressed this way:

Ephesians 5:21-25—and be subject to one another in the fear of Messiah. Wives, be subject to your own husbands, as to the Lord, For the husband is the head of the wife, as Messiah also is the head of the congregation, He Himself being the Savior of the body. But as the congregation is subject to Messiah, so also the wives ought to be to their husbands in everything. Husbands love your wives, just as Messiah also loved the congregation and gave Himself up for her.

If God uses the marriage relationship to describe His love for Israel and for the body of Messiah, we need to take note and understand the importance of respecting marriage and the idea of having a husband. Whether you are presently married, have never been married, or have been married and are now divorced, you need to be on God's side when it comes to supporting marriages.

Marriage is serious business for God, and in Malachi, He tells Israel how odious divorce is in His eyes:

> Malachi 2:14-16—Yet you say, for what reason? Because the LORD has been a witness between you and the wife of your youth, against whom you have dealt treacherously, though she is your companion and your wife by covenant. But not one has done so who has a remnant of the Spirit. And what did that one do while he was seeking a godly offspring? Take heed then to your spirit, and let no one deal treacherously against the wife of your youth. For *I hate divorce*, says the LORD, the God of Israel, and him who covers his garment with wrong, says the LORD of hosts. So take heed to your spirit, that you do not deal treacherously.

In the New Covenant, Messiah reiterates this teaching as He instructs the Pharisees about divorce saying, "For this cause a man shall leave his father and mother, and shall cleave to his wife; and the two shall become one flesh. For this reason they are no longer two, but one flesh. What therefore God has joined together let no man separate" (Matthew 19:5-6).

With divorce so rampant in the United States in both the secular and believing communities, we need to instruct younger women about whom to marry and why.

My Own Search

Why is it important to marry not just a believer but a committed believer? I'd like to share a personal testimony about "how I found my husband" that I hope will be an encouragement, especially to those young ladies who are looking to get married.

Even as a committed believer who was involved in full time ministry, I made a number of mistakes in my past relationships. I seemed to get crushes on cute guys that would zap my focus from what the Lord wanted me to do. When I lived in Israel, I was especially vulnerable to these crushes. Please, don't get me wrong. I wasn't outwardly immoral, and by God's grace, I did manage to have an effective witness and ministry in Israel. After I returned to New York City, the dating and the crushes continued. However, the Lord began to speak to my heart, and I started to pray differently.

Dear Lord, I know You love me and want the very best for my life. If You want me to minister as a single woman, I yield myself to You. I want Your will for my life also to be my will. In fact, I am so tired of dating and trying to figure this out, I don't really want to date anymore. If there is a guy that You want me to marry, please have this man know that I am the one for him. And, Lord, since You have called me to minister and communicate Good News, please have this man not only have a passion for You but the same burden for Israel that You have given me. Thanks! In Yeshua's Name. Amen.

Well, that was my prayer, and guess what? God answered it in a wonderful way. When I first met Sam, on a visit to San Francisco, he was a new believer about a week old in the Lord. But a year later when I returned to live and minister in San Francisco, Sam was in Bible College and on fire for the Lord. We traveled together with an evangelistic music team, *The Liberated Wailing Wall*, and even in those early days, I could see that Sam had a gift of evangelism which I respected. One day he asked me for a date. I told him I was busy, as I had a Hebrew folk music class and then an Israeli dance class on the Berkeley campus. He quickly informed me that he loved music as well as Jewish folk dancing!

Our next two dates consisted of handing out evangelistic tracts and going for coffee afterwards. On our third date, as Sam was taking me to my apartment, he told me, "Miriam, I'm going to marry you." My first response was to laugh. But as I began praying about Sam's proposal, I remembered my prayer to the Lord and thanked Him for bringing a decisive, passionate believer into my life. That was in November of 1972. In June of 1973, we were married and have continued serving the Lord together since then.

Ladies, don't short change yourselves. God has some great advice for us if we only listen. He knows you better than you know yourself, and your Creator can bring the right person into your life so that you can serve Him together.

But if your purpose in getting married is to have your husband meet your needs, then you will be sorely disappointed. He may be sincere when he promises, "Sweetheart, I will meet your every need!" But you would be naive to believe a promise that could only be fulfilled by God.

Can A Husband Meet My Needs?

Even though Sam is a wonderful husband, I had to learn that he could not meet the deepest longings of my heart. After a few years of growing in the Lord and in our marriage, I began to understand that first I had to have the Lord fill my life, and the overflow would minister to the life of my husband. He found out the same thing: that as we served the Lord together and grew in Him, our marriage was a testimony to what He alone could provide.

Keeping in mind that only the Lord - not your husband - can fulfill your deepest needs. Let's take a look at 2 Corinthians 6, where Paul gives a number of excellent reasons why they and we too, should not be unequally joined to those who do not believe. This joining may refer to business agreements or other partnerships, but of all of the unions that you can think of, is not marriage the most serious and lasting?

In taking a closer look at the passage, we see Paul's heart for those to whom he is writing. He speaks to them as a father would speak to his children. What advice does he have for them? Paul tells them not to be joined to those who are unbelievers.

Paul presents a list of contrasts for us to examine:

> 2 Corinthians 6:14-18—Do not be bound together with unbelievers, for what partnership have righteousness and lawlessness, or what fellowship has light with darkness? Or what harmony has Messiah with Belial, or what has a believer in common with an unbeliever? Or what agreement has the temple of God with idols? For we are the temple of the living God; just as God said, I will dwell in them and walk among them; and I will be their God, and they shall be My people. Therefore, come out from their midst and be separate, says the Lord. And do not touch what is unclean; and I will welcome you. And I will be a father to you, and you shall be sons and daughters to Me, says the Lord Almighty.

Let's take a closer look at this list of opposite pairs. The questions are:

- *How can a believer and an unbeliever be bound together?* In marriage, man and woman become one flesh—*basar echad*. This is designated as "leaving and cleaving." "For this cause a man shall leave his father and his mother, and shall cleave to his wife; and they shall become one flesh" (Genesis 22:24). God's plan is for you and your husband to have the most intimate of relationships. How can a godly relationship be truly intimate if your spouse does not believe in your God?

- *What partnership does righteousness have with lawlessness?* How can you agree on common values? Amos 3:3 says, "How can two walk together, unless they are agreed?" Those who are not under God's law are without law.

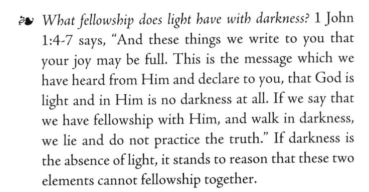

- *What fellowship does light have with darkness?* 1 John 1:4-7 says, "And these things we write to you that your joy may be full. This is the message which we have heard from Him and declare to you, that God is light and in Him is no darkness at all. If we say that we have fellowship with Him, and walk in darkness, we lie and do not practice the truth." If darkness is the absence of light, it stands to reason that these two elements cannot fellowship together.

- *What harmony do Messiah and Belial have together?* Belial, in the Greek, is a name for Satan. Paul is asking how the King of Kings can agree with the prince of darkness, the one who rebelled and was thrown out of the heavenly kingdom.

- *What does a believer have in common with an unbeliever?* The believer's life is based on God's values, and the unbeliever's life is based on the world's values, so how can they have anything in common?

- *How can the temple of God agree with idols?* Romans 12:1 says, "I beseech you therefore, brethren, by the mercies of God, that you present your bodies a living sacrifice, holy, acceptable to God, which is your reasonable service." We are the temple of the living God. How can we present ourselves as a living sacrifice if our husband is a worshiper of idols?

It is vital to understand God's view of marriage. He declared this covenant relationship so that a man and a woman could live in intimacy and love, reflecting His greater intimacy and His greater love. We must understand that getting married is a choice each of us is free to make. God is not going to love us more or less if we are married.

It is folly to think that we can enter into marriage without our primary relationship with God in focus. My marriage is successful to the degree that my relationship with God is successful when I am drawing on His strength, His wisdom, and His loving kindness.

THOUGHT QUESTIONS

1. Will marriage meet my needs as a person?

2. Will having a husband fulfill my life?

3. How can I be a "husband lover" if I am single, widowed, or in the loveless marriage?

4. How does today's society influence your perception of marriage?

5. How does your marriage experience shape your view of marriage in contrast to God's view?

6. Since people change, mature, and grow, does it really matter whom I will marry?

RECOMMENDATIONS

+ It will be helpful to memorize a verse that reminds you that the Lord can meet all of your needs regardless of your situation in life, for example, Psalm 23:1 and Colossians 2:10.

+ Pray for specific marriages around you and in the congregation, that God may be honored in those homes.

+ Is there a young woman you can encourage? Begin praying for her and for the opportunity to minister to her.

Her children rise up and bless her.

Proverbs 31:28

Chapter 3

GOD'S VIEW OF CHILDREN

INHERITANCE FROM THE LORD

These passages from *What Our Mothers Didn't Tell Us* by Danielle Crittenden captures the essence of how secular society views children and motherhood.

> As modern women, we are taught to anticipate many things in our lives—except one…. We plot every move advancing career as carefully and thoughtfully as a cartographer. But the single most profound life-changing decision that the majority of us eventually make is the one we are least prepared for—the act of having a child! The contemporary wisdom of modern society teaches us to be wary of motherhood—to fit motherhood into our careers and to "do it when it's convenient" and "to not let it define you." The discovery when we do have babies, of course, is that they in no way "fit into" any career, that they can never be described as "convenient," and that motherhood is about as defining an experience as any human being can undergo. For more than thirty years the women's movement has told us that we would be happier, more fulfilled human beings, if we left our homes and children and went out to work.

To the degree that we might feel misgivings or guilt about leaving our babies to others to raise, we have been assured that such feelings are imposed upon us by society.... Instead, we have been taught to suppress these worries and to put our work ahead of our families, or at the very least, to attempt to "balance" the demands of boss and baby. Any strong rush of maternal feeling, any desire to surrender pieces of our professional selves, is viewed as a reversion to some stereotype of motherhood the women's movement was supposed to have emancipated us from. The popular books on motherhood being written by feminists today are no less vehement than they were in 1972 that full-time motherhood is a servile and ultimately dangerous state for women to succumb to. Being a good mother, they say, means taking care of ourselves first and learning to let "others" needs come second.

The opening comments of this chapter illustrate how important it is for us as older women to make an impact upon the women we mentor and disciple. We need to teach this generation God's view of motherhood and children

We learned that the phrase, "to love their husbands" does not have the pronoun in the Greek but was rather a compound word that literally meant "husband-lovers." The same grammatical structure is used in the Greek for "to love (their) children." This phrase combines *phileo*, love, with the word *teknos* or children: *philoteknos*, or literally *children-lovers*.

> Titus 2:3-4—Older women likewise are to be reverent in their behavior, not malicious gossips, nor enslaved to much wine, teaching what is good, that they may encourage (*put in their right mind*) the young women to love (*their*) husbands (*philandros*), to love (*their*) children (*philoteknos*).

Being A Children-Lover

The quality of being a "children-lover" reveals God's point of view concerning children. God's will for us is to disciple younger women regarding the value He places on children. The Lord wants us to understand how He builds and influences society through our families. But contemporary society portrays a different and largely demeaning view of motherhood and child-rearing.

Let us therefore begin where we should always begin when there is a cataclysmic difference between the Word of God and the philosophical views of contemporary society. We must ask ourselves, "What is God's view of the home and of children? How does God expect us to build homes?"

God's blueprint for a family

Psalm 127 is the middle Song of Ascent written by King Solomon and sung or recited by the pilgrims as they went up to Jerusalem to celebrate the various Feasts of the Lord. Let's take a closer look at the first three verses:

> Psalm 127:1-3—Unless the LORD builds the house, they labor in vain who build it; unless the LORD guards the city, the watchman keeps awake in vain. It is vain for you to rise up early, to retire late, to eat the bread of painful labors; for He gives to His beloved even in his sleep. Behold, children are a gift of the LORD; the fruit of the womb is a reward.

The first verse says that if God does not build our homes, we will find our labor to be empty and fruitless. But how does God build?

The Hebrew word for build is *banah*. From the same root used in "build" we get a family of words including the words for son—*ben* and daughter *bat*. Some of you may be familiar with the terms *Bar-Mitzvah*, (son or *ben* of the commandment), or *Bat-Mitzvah*, daughter of the commandment. These are special confirmation ceremonies for sons (age 13) and daughters (age 12) in both traditional and messianic Jewish communities. The same Hebrew root is also found in the word for house (*bayith*). God builds His homes through sons and daughters, not brick and wood. But unless He is the principal builder, all of the work is in vain.

OUR DIVINE ARCHITECT

These Scriptures challenge me. Do they speak to you? Are you letting the Lord build your home, as you acknowledge that your children are an inheritance and blessing from God? It is only through God's blessing that you can build your home and be protected by the Lord.

Verse one also states that the Lord is the protector and security for the family. He keeps, watches, and preserves. The Hebrew word for watchman is *shamar* and is used twice in this verse for the words guard and watchman. "Unless the LORD *guards* the city, The *watchman* keeps awake in vain." The Lord is the One who gives security to the family and to the community. We should also note that if the Lord does not give success, it will all be in vain; the building (home) will fall. If God is not the builder of the home, then we labor in vain.

In Psalm 121, the theme that God is our protector and our security is repeated and reiterated.

> Psalm 121:1-8—I will lift up my eyes to the mountains; from whence shall my help come? My help comes from the LORD, Who made heaven and earth. He will not allow your foot to slip; He who *keeps* you will not slumber. Behold, He who *keeps* Israel will neither slumber nor sleep. The LORD is your *keeper*; The LORD is your shade on your right hand. The sun will not smite you by day, nor the moon by night. The LORD will *protect* you from all evil; He will *keep* your soul. The LORD will *guard* your going out and your coming in from this time forth and forever.

OUR HEAVENLY WATCHMAN

Notice that the word "guard" (*shamar*) is used six times in eight verses. From repetitive use of the word, we can understand where our true help comes. It comes from the One who is our Creator (v. 2). If He is your protector, He will keep you in the same manner that He watches over Israel. I am so thankful for this verse that assures us that our God does not slumber or sleep! When I'm worrying in the middle of the night, I like to remember that I'm not alone and cast my worry on the One who is always awake and watching over me. We do not have a God that slumbers, but a God who watches over and protects His flock.

Because God is the only One who can give us real security for ourselves, our children, and our homes, the question is, "Do you allow Him to secure you, your husband, and your children?"

OUR LASTING LEGACY

Psalm 127:3 says, "Behold, children are a gift of the LORD; the fruit of the womb is a reward." This verse gives us God's view of children. It begins with a strong word that demands our attention. In Hebrew, *hine* or "behold" is like yelling, "Listen to this" "Pay attention; I'm going to say something wonderful!" (Isaiah 7:14 and Psalm 133:1 are two other places where this word is used).

The Psalmist says, "children are a gift from the Lord." The word *nachalah* means gift, heritage, or inheritance. A heritage is something acquired or descended from a predecessor, a legacy. In other words, these children are not merely gifts like a present to be opened at a birthday celebration. Children are from the Lord and our inheritance, intended to make an impact upon their world. Sam, my husband, taught the following from Psalm 127:

> Children are an inheritance belonging to the Lord. They are our stewardship in the Lord. We are the managers, not the owners. We need to see children as God sees them. Each child is a transfer of God's love from His heart to your family. We have great kids if we trust that a great God has given them to us. Great kings give great gifts! We don't want merely natural children, but we want to have spiritual children. Your children will grow into greatness by the kind of investment you make into them. Successful families see their kids as a heritage from God and care for them as such.

In the last two verses of Psalm 127, we see this idea of making impact upon society. The Psalmist compares children to arrows in the hands of a warrior.

Having children make their mark on society is similar to a warrior hitting his target with an arrow. Psalm 127:4-5 says, "Like arrows in the hand of a warrior, so are the children of one's youth. How blessed is the man whose quiver is full of them; they shall not be ashamed, when they speak with their enemies in the gate." But what does it mean that "the fruit of the womb is a reward?" To have a family in Jewish society was a blessing; not to have one was considered a curse. We see in the following verses that children come from the Lord. Notice how Jacob responds to a frustrated Rachel who threatens her husband, saying that she will die if he doesn't give her children! How does Jacob answer his wife? He says, in Genesis 30:2b, *Am I in the place of God*, who has withheld from you the fruit of the womb?"

In Genesis 33, we find two brothers, Esau and Jacob, who are seeing each other again after a number of years. When Esau sees all of the people with Jacob, he asks him, "Who do these belong to?" Jacob acknowledges that they are children who were graciously given to him by the Lord. Genesis 33:5 says, "And he (Esau) lifted his eyes and saw the women and the children, and said, 'Who are these with you?' So he (Jacob) said, *'the children whom God has graciously given* your servant.'"

Joseph desired the blessing of his earthly father Jacob for his children. Joseph acknowledged, as well, that his two sons, (Manasseh and Ephraim), were given to him by God.

Genesis 48:9 — And Joseph said to his father, "they are my sons, whom *God has given me here.*" So he said, 'Bring them to me, please, that I may bless them'"

Your reward shall be very great

Children are a gift from the Lord, and the fruit of the womb is a reward, "wages" or *sakar*.

The word "reward" or *sakar* is a special word. It does not mean that God is paying us to have kids, but it does mean that our labor is not in vain in the Lord. This word is used in wonderful ways that should encourage our hearts. Genesis 15:1 says, "After these things the word of the LORD came to Abram in a vision, saying, 'Do not fear, Abram, I am a shield to you; your *reward* shall be very great.'"

In speaking of the coming of Messiah, Scripture proclaims in Isaiah 40:10, "Behold, the Lord God will come with might, with His arm ruling for Him. Behold, His *reward* is with Him, and His recompense before Him." Use of the word *reward* in reference to the Messiah also occurs in Isaiah 62:11, "Behold, the LORD has proclaimed to the end of the earth, Say to the daughter of Zion, 'Lo, your salvation comes; behold His *reward* is with Him, and His recompense before Him.'" And again in Proverbs 11:18, "The wicked earns deceptive wages, but he who sows righteousness gets a true *reward*."

Point of dedication

Psalm 127:3a tells us that children, according to God's building plan, are an inheritance from Him. The next phrase gives us an idea of what we are to do with these gifts (children). Proverbs 22:6 says, "*Train up* a child in the way he should go, even when he is old he will not depart from it."

What does it mean "to train"? The Hebrew word, *chanak*, means to train up, dedicate. The root of this word is found in the holiday called *Hanukkah* or the Feast of Dedication (John 10:22).

How do we make our children disciples? We give them unconditional love and consistent training. The word *dedicate* or train is also used to describe the disciples of Abram who helped him defeat the kings who had captured his nephew, Lot. Genesis 14:14 says, "And when Abram heard that his relative had been taken captive, he led out his *trained* men, born in his house, three hundred eighteen, and went in pursuit as far as Dan."

These three hundred eighteen dedicated men did not come from Abram's own loins. The point is they were born in his house and had been discipled, trained, and dedicated by Abram so he could trust them with an important and difficult task.

We are instructed to teach our children. Every week many of us recite the *Sh'ma* (the passage from Deuteronomy 6:4-8) which emphasizes that we are to teach, train, and disciple the next generation.

> Deuteronomy 6:4-9—Hear, O Israel! The LORD is our God, the LORD is one! And you shall love the LORD your God with all your heart and with all your soul and with all your might. And these words, which I am commanding you today, shall be on your heart; and you shall teach them diligently to your sons and shall talk of them when you sit in your house and when you walk by the way and when you lie down and when you rise up. And you shall bind them as a sign on your hand

and they shall be as frontals on your forehead. And you shall write them on the doorposts of your house and on your gates.

This training is something that is done for a child or new believer, to help them grow. Young children as well as young believers need consistent discipline.

Proverbs 23:13; 22-25—Do not hold back discipline from the child, although you strike him with the rod, he will not die. Listen to your father who begot you, and do not despise your mother when she is old. Buy truth, and do not sell it, get wisdom and instruction and understanding. The father of the righteous will greatly rejoice, and he who begets a wise son will be glad in him. Let your father and your mother be glad, and let her rejoice who gave birth to you.

However, it is not just about having physical children. God has called us to disciple these gifts so they have an impact on the world around them. This is a calling to discipleship for both our physical and our spiritual children. All believers in Messiah can bear fruit through discipleship. But unless you depend upon the Lord to raise your children, whether physical or spiritual, there will be no eternal rewards.

This discipleship takes time and commitment. It's like teaching the art of brushing one's teeth. When my son had his first few teeth appear, I did not sit him down and give him an hour lecture on the importance of dental hygiene, nor did I wait until he was old enough to walk to the sink, give him his own toothbrush, and tell him to figure out this oral hygiene himself.

No, I took my young son to the sink (sometimes under great protest) and showed him how to brush his teeth, demonstrating and taking him through the steps. And I made sure that this became a daily part of his life, lest he end up with a mouth full of cavities.

This is what God wants us to do with our children, whether they are physical or spiritual: to take them line by line, precept by precept, through the Word of God. This leads to understanding and spiritual maturity, and a spiritually mature person is a well-trained person who is dedicated to the Lord.

As we desire to have our lives count for God, how do we produce fruit? It says "the fruit of the womb is a reward" (Psalm 127:3b). The physical fruit is a gift. Scripture also tells us how we can produce lasting fruit.

Such fruit can only be produced one way. Messiah said to His disciples, "Abide in Me, and I in you. As the branch cannot bear fruit of itself, unless it abides in the vine, so neither can you, unless you abide in Me" (John 15:4).

In chapter four we will meet a woman from the pages of Scripture who understood God's heart for children.

THOUGHT QUESTIONS

1. How do you view children in general?

2. How do you see the children in your family?

3. In light of this chapter, do you need to reevaluate your view of children and their role in society?

4. Are you making disciples for the Lord?

5. What legacy are you leaving behind?

6. Are you investing in your children/disciples so you will reap eternal dividends?

7. Abraham trained and discipled men he could depend on in the difficult times. Are you?

*A Virtuous Woman girds herself
with strength and makes
her arms strong.*

Proverbs 31:17

Chapter 4

A Desire Fulfilled

Hannah Understood The High Value of Children

In the previous chapter, we noted that in Psalm 127:3 the phrase "the fruit of the womb is a reward" emphasized the importance of having children in ancient Jewish society. To have a family was a blessing; not to have one was seen as a curse.

To understand this concept, let's look at the life of one of my heroes in Scripture. But prior to introducing her, let me pose a few questions for your consideration:

- Are you dealing with a disappointment - perhaps even anger and frustration - over a situation that you have committed to prayer?

- Do you believe that God will give you the desires of your heart?

- Do you ever feel that God is not answering your prayers?

- Are you insecure about who you are?

- Do you have people hassling you and making you feel badly about yourself?

- Did God forget to give you what you need to succeed in this world?

If you can answer yes to some of these questions, then get ready to learn from one of the greatest gals of Israel! Her name is Hannah, and her story is found in the first two chapters of 1 Samuel.

Loved and despised

We know from her husband's actions and comments that Hannah had his love and respect, "but to Hannah he (Elkanah) would give a double portion, for he loved Hannah, but the LORD had closed her womb. Then Elkanah her husband said to her, Hannah, why do you weep and why do you not eat and why is your heart sad? Am I not better to you than ten sons?" (1 Samuel 1:5, 8).

But Hannah was childless because "the Lord had closed her womb" (1 Samuel 1:6). Since children were known as a blessing from the Lord and it clearly states in Scripture that God closed Hannah's womb, Hannah perceived her childless condition as a curse.

She had plenty of help in this, because "her *rival* (Peninnah), would *provoke* her bitterly *to irritate* her, because the LORD had closed Hannah's womb" (1 Samuel 1:6).

In order to understand fully Hannah's difficulties, we must examine three Hebrew words from verse six.

The first word describes Peninnah by saying she was Hannah's rival. The Hebrew word for "rival" is *tsarah*, which means distress, trouble, or vexer. Perhaps some of you know this word in another context, because this Hebrew word *tsarah* is also the root of a common Yiddish expression: *tzoros* or troubles. From *The Vocabulary of Jewish Life* by Abraham Heller, he gives an explanation of the Yiddish expression *tzoros*:

> There is no easy answer to the question why man suffers. Among the many explanations given by Judaism two stand out: If you desire life, you must expect suffering or *tsoros*. One without the other is not possible. Second, suffering is known in Jewish tradition as *Yesurim shel Ahavah*—chastisement of love. Man is purified and ennobled by troubles. He who never suffers can have no sympathy for the trouble (*tzoros*).

The word *tsarah* is used about seventy times in the Hebrew Scriptures. One example is in Psalm 91:15, "He will call upon Me, and I will answer him; I will be with him in *trouble*; I will rescue him, and honor him."

In Psalm 22 (the prophecy and description of Messiah's death on the cross), the word *tsarah* is used in verse 11. "Be not far from me, for *trouble* is near; for there is none to help."

When the wayward prophet Jonah was praying from the belly of the great fish, he said, "I called out of my *distress* to the LORD, and He answered me. I cried for help from the depth of Sheol; Thou didst hear my voice" (Jonah 2:2).

TROUBLE WITH A CAPITAL T

Peninnah was *trouble* for Hannah. It seems that the term "rival" wife could be translated as one who brings distress and trouble. We see this further developed in the word provoke.

In Hebrew the word for "provoke" is *kaas*, which means to provoke to anger, demoralize, or spite. One common usage for provoke (*kaas*) is found in the phrase *"provoking the Lord"* to describe what Israel as a nation or a certain King in Israel did when they would forsake the Lord. It was a terrible sin to provoke the Lord and incur His judgment. Two examples are found in Judges and 2 Kings.

> Judges 2:12—and they (Israel) forsook the LORD, the God of their fathers, who had brought them out of the land of Egypt, and followed other gods from among the gods of the peoples who were around them, and bowed themselves down to them; thus they *provoked the LORD* to anger.

> 2 Kings 17:11—and there they (Israel) burned incense on all the high places as the nations did which the LORD had carried away to exile before them; and they did evil things *provoking the LORD.*

I wonder if Peninnah provoked the Lord as she vented her bitterness and resentment upon Hannah, God's servant.

Do we ever provoke the Lord by venting our bitterness and anger against His servants? When our pride is hurt, do we turn our back on Him and act in accordance with our fleshly desires?

Another usage of provoke (*kaas*) is found in Proverbs 27:3 where it says, "A stone is heavy and the sand weighty, but the *provocation* of a fool is heavier than both of them." Relating this to Hannah's situation, we may be able to empathize with her. How awful this provocation and grief must have been, coming from the rival who was trouble personified.

This word *kaas* or "provoke" in 1 Samuel 1:6 is used in 1 Samuel 1:7 and 1:16

> 1 Samuel 1:7—And it happened year after year, as often as she went up to the house of the LORD, she would *provoke* her, so she wept and would not eat.

> 1 Samuel 1:16 —Do not consider your maidservant as a worthless woman; for I have spoken until now out of my great concern and *provocation*.

Verse 7 says that as often as Hannah would go up to worship the Lord, Peninnah would provoke her. So Peninnah's demoralizing, angry, and spiteful behavior was not only constant, it also increased in intensity when Hannah would go up to Shiloh to worship the Lord.

What do you think Peninnah's motivation might have been? Was she jealous of her husband's love for Hannah? Was she envious of Hannah's love for the God of Israel, making her want to accuse and demoralize her faith? How odious Peninnah's behavior must have been to God.

Have you ever been so disappointed, so grief stricken, that your stomach was upset and in knots to the extent that you were unable to eat?

Look at verse 6, which gives us an even deeper understanding of what Hannah was going through, "so she wept and would not eat."

But the third Hebrew word gives us even further insight. In some of the English versions for 1 Samuel 1:6 it says, "Her rival (*tsara* or trouble), however, would provoke her bitterly *kaas* or bring her to grief to irritate her, because the LORD had closed her womb."

The word *kaas* (provoke or bring to grief) is repeated in this verse; the second time it is connected to the English words *to irritate* her. When I think of something irritating me, it is usually something small, like the music is being played too loudly, or I get caught in a traffic jam when running late. However, the Hebrew is much stronger!

How did Peninnah's anger, vexation, and provocation affect or irritate Hannah? Let's look at the verse again. Peninnah "would provoke her bitterly *to irritate (raam)* her, because the LORD had closed her womb" (1 Samuel 1:6).

This Hebrew word *raam* means to thunder, roar, rage, or cause to tremble. Think of how you feel when you hear thunder. I want to run and hide. Thunder is not only intrusive, it is frightening. It can be overwhelming as the thunder gets closer and closer.

This same Hebrew word *raam* is found in the next chapter as part of Hannah's prayer. 1 Samuel 2:10 says, "those who contend with the LORD will be shattered; against them He will *thunder (raam)* in the heavens, the LORD will judge the ends of the earth; and He will give strength to His king, and will exalt the horn of His anointed."

Once again we are given a picture of Hannah's disturbing predicament. She faced the stigma placed on her by society, great personal disappointment, and undue persecution from her rival (child-bearing) wife.

Grief poured out by a humble servant

Hannah was brought out of this adversity through bitter heartache and trial by depending solely on the Lord. As she faithfully went to Shiloh to worship the Lord, she learned that the secret to deal with bitterness is a close personal relationship with God. 1 Samuel 1:10 says of Hannah, "And she was in bitterness of soul, and prayed to the LORD and wept in anguish" (NKJ). The term "bitterness of soul" uses two Hebrew words that mean bitterness (*mara* - think of the *moror* or bitter herbs at Passover) of soul (*nefesh*).

It was out of her distress that Hannah answered when Eli accused her of being drunk with wine.

> 1 Samuel 1:15-16—No, my lord, I am a woman oppressed in spirit. I have drunk neither wine nor strong drink, but I have poured out my soul *before the Lord*. Do not consider your maidservant as a worthless woman; for I have spoken until now out of my great concern and provocation.

"Before the Lord" literally means to the face of God. As Hannah continues to speak to Eli, she exhorts him. Remember that Eli was a priest who ministered in the time of the Judges, a spiritually low time for Israel where "everyone did what was right in his own eyes" (Judges 21:25).

It was probably unusual for Eli to see such sincere prayer from a godly woman. In her response to Eli, Hannah tells him that she is not ungodly or worthless, but rather a handmaid or female servant.

In calling herself a female servant or slave, she demonstrates humility. It amazes me to think that God used Hannah to encourage Eli the priest. Even in her weakened, grief stricken condition, she was able to speak God's truth to Eli and exhort him to trust the Lord, as she prayed and poured out her heart to God.

Here we see an intimate picture of Hannah coming into the presence of the living God and pouring out the bitterness and distress of her soul. This is exactly what God desires that we do continually. When distress, heartache, resentment, or other strife resulting from life's disappointments enters your life and seeks to overtake your soul, run to the Lord. Pour out your heart to Him, and let His peace fill you.

Notice Eli's response to Hannah's faithful prayer, found in 1 Samuel 1:17, "Then Eli answered and said, 'Go in peace; and may the God of Israel grant your petition that you have asked of Him.'" Eli remembers that he is a servant of the Most High God and has compassion on Hannah. He joins her in her prayer need as he tells her to go in shalom (peace).

For many of us, *shalom* is a common word of greeting, but it also means completeness and wholeness. Using this phrase, Eli was telling Hannah that, whatever happened, her completeness or wholeness could be found in her trust in the God of Israel.

ANOTHER BROKEN VESSEL

David could have related to Hannah's grief. He knew what it felt like to be in great distress:

> Psalm 31:9-13—Be gracious to me, O LORD, for I am in distress. My eye is wasted away from *grief* (*kaas*), my soul and my body also. For my life is spent with sorrow, and my years with sighing; my strength has failed because of my iniquity, and my body has wasted away. Because of all my adversaries, I have become a reproach, especially to my neighbors, and an object of dread to my acquaintances; those who see me in the street flee from me. I am forgotten as a dead man, out of mind, I am like a broken vessel. For I have heard the slander of many, terror is on every side; while they took counsel together against me, they schemed to take away my life.

Like Hannah, David understood that no matter what was coming upon him - even if he felt invisible, crushed and broken, with slander on every side, he could trust the Lord to deliver him. In the Psalms, he acknowledges that his times and circumstances are in the very hands of God. He is assured of God's deliverance, His intimate presence and His tender mercies. David says with confidence, "But as for me, I trust in Thee, O LORD, I say, thou art my God. My times are in Thy hand; deliver me from the hand of my enemies, and from those who persecute me. Make Thy face to shine upon thy servant; save me in Thy lovingkindness." (Psalm 31:14-16)

Like David and Hannah, we can have this confidence and trust in the Lord when our times get tough!

My times are in Thy hand

Hannah poured out her heart to the Lord. Her request was for a son who she would give back to God to be His servant. In the Hebrew, the words requests, petitions, and desires are from the same root (*shaal*). It is used in Psalm 37:4, "Delight yourself in the LORD; and he will give you the *desires* of your heart."

Hannah had already told Eli that she was a humble servant of God, and that in light of this love for the Lord, she did not want motherhood in order to feel good about herself or to complete her by possessing a child. She understood that children would be a "gift or inheritance" from the Lord and that their purpose was to bring glory to the God of Israel.

When Eli answered Hannah, he said, "Go in peace; and may the God of Israel grant your *petition* that you have *asked (shaal)* of Him" (1 Samuel 1:17). Eli encouraged her, and Hannah responded, "Let your maidservant find favor in your sight" (1 Samuel 1:18). Hannah went her way and ate, and her face was no longer sad. Hannah, whose name means "gracious one," indeed found grace in the eyes of God and Eli.

How could Hannah trust the Lord with her situation, which had been causing her constant grief?

The circumstances had not changed. When she returned home, the *trouble* (Peninnah) would continue to provoke her. What would be different?

The difference was that she had poured out her heart and soul to the Lord. She did not pretend that everything was OK or put on a "happy face."

She presented her problem to God, and although she had no idea how the situation would come to fruition, she had Eli's blessing and her husband's support. Above all, she had an intimate relationship with the God of Israel, and she knew that she could trust Him implicitly.

THE PRAYER THAT GOD HEARS

The result of Hannah's prayer was that God heard and gave her the desires of her heart! Do you believe He listens to you and works on your behalf?

My husband, Sam's verse-by-verse exposition of Romans chapter 8 helped to change the way I approach my prayer life and taught me to bring my desires before the Lord.

> Romans 8:26-27—And in the same way the Spirit also helps our weakness; for we do not know how to pray as we should, but the Spirit Himself intercedes for us with groanings too deep for words; and He who searches the hearts knows what the mind of the Spirit is, because He intercedes for the saints according to the will of God.

Paul is teaching us that even if we do not know exactly how to pray for things, the Holy Spirit of God does. He is interceding for me with "groanings deeper than words." The Holy Spirit knows the will of the Lord!

Sam's illustration helped me to understand this idea. When we would take our very young son out for lunch, he sometimes wanted to order on his own, saying to the waitress, "I would like an ice cream sundae and cookies for lunch." As his loving parents, we would say to the waitress, "What our son means to say is that he would like a chicken sandwich on whole wheat bread with a glass of juice."

Because of our love for our son, we would reinterpret his request to the waitress in order to make it something good and wholesome that would ultimately be the best for him.

There are many times when I do not know what the will of the Lord is for a particular situation. However, if I trust in Him and yield my heart to Him, I can be assured that He knows what the best is for me. As Romans 8:28 says, "And we know that God causes all things to work together for good to those who love God, to those who are called according to His purpose."

When God answered Hannah's prayer and gave her a son, Hannah kept her promise to God and dedicated Samuel (which means "heard of God") to the Lord. God rewarded Hannah's faithfulness, and she saw Samuel become a mighty leader in Israel. She had her priorities straight. God had given her the desire to seek Him. God used her grief and distress to change Hannah's heart, which she yielded unto the Lord.

A HEART OVERFLOWS WITH PRAISE

In thanksgiving, Hannah pens this incredible prayer of praise. From Hannah's prayer in Chapter 2 we see an amazing account of who her God is and what He alone can do.

1 Samuel 2:1-10—Then Hannah prayed and said, my heart exults in the LORD; my horn is exalted in the LORD, my mouth speaks boldly against my enemies, because I rejoice in Thy salvation. There is no one holy like the LORD, indeed, there is no one besides Thee, nor is there any rock like our God.

Boast no more so very proudly, do not let arrogance come out of your mouth; for the LORD is a God of knowledge, and with Him actions are weighed. The bows of the mighty are shattered, but the feeble gird on strength. Those who were full hire themselves out for bread, but those who were hungry cease to hunger. Even the barren gives birth to seven, but she who has many children languishes. The LORD kills and makes alive; He brings down to Sheol and raises up. The LORD makes poor and rich; He brings low, He also exalts. He raises the poor from the dust, He lifts the needy from the ash heap to make them sit with nobles, and inherit a seat of honor; for the pillars of the earth are the LORD's, and He set the world on them. He keeps the feet of His godly ones, but the wicked ones are silenced in darkness; for not by might shall a man prevail. Those who contend with the LORD will be shattered; against them He will thunder in the heavens, the LORD will judge the ends of the earth; and He will give strength to His king, and will exalt the horn of His anointed.

In verse 1, we see that her prayer originates from the heart - a heart that rejoices in the Lord. Her "horn" (which means "strength") was magnified and lifted up in her God. She could speak with confidence against her enemies to the Lord. Why? Because she was rejoicing in God's salvation. She knew that she could find her joy and her strength in the God of Israel.

In this amazing prayer, she also explains the character of her God who brings her salvation. In verse 2, she talks about God's uniqueness: He is Holy (*kadosh*). He alone is worthy of praise and adoration.

He is the Rock, our stability through every circumstance of life. Hannah was focusing her life on the Lord and building her life upon the Rock, are you?

In verse 3, Hannah goes on to proclaim that God is all knowing or omniscient: "a God of knowledge." God is truly a "know it all." Do you believe this? Are you convinced that God is totally aware of your desires, your needs, your heart?

The Lord is also all-powerful or omnipotent. He weighs and measures every action. In other words, nobody gets away with anything.

Therefore, we must believe that God is in control of all our circumstances. Do you believe that God can completely take care of your situation?

Verses 4 through 9 give a series of contrasts between those who trust God and those who do not:

+ Verse 4: mighty or feeble

+ Verse 5: satisfied or hungry

+ Verse 5: fruitful or barren

+ Verse 6: alive or dead

+ Verse 6: high or low

+ Verse 7: rich or poor

+ Verses 8 and 9: security or defeat

In this list we see that God turns things around. Those who are rich and look well-fed and satisfied can be spiritually poor, starving, and barren. They may even be the "walking dead."

They appear as though everything is fine, but on the inside there is no life, no security, and no strength.

This list could be a checklist for you. If you trust in the Lord, then you will have the victory. If you trust in yourself and your strength, you will be defeated.

Where do you stand? Think about Peninnah and where she would fit into this list. She felt superior and fruitful and took every chance she could to cause Hannah trouble. But Hannah was able to have victory in a persistently difficult situation because she poured out her heart to the Lord and trusted Him alone for the outcome.

Her dedication of Samuel to the Lord helps us to understand the value of loving children. Hannah understood how important children are to God. She knew that if she dedicated her son to the Lord for His service, the sacrifice of having Samuel live at the Temple from his young years on would be worth it. She understood that God can use a child to influence the world. Samuel became a great prophet in Israel.

In the final verse of Hannah's prayer she says, "those who contend with the LORD will be shattered; against them He will thunder in the heavens, the LORD will judge the ends of the earth; and He will give strength to His king, and will exalt the horn of His anointed" (1 Samuel 2:10).

Samuel had the privilege of anointing David, the greatest king of Israel, through whom an even greater King would come, God's anointed Messiah (*Mashiach*).

After chapter one of 1 Samuel, Peninnah is not mentioned again. But even as Samuel was growing in the Lord to be a leader among his people, Hannah was blessed by God with more children. 1 Samuel 2:21 confirms this, "And the LORD visited Hannah; and she conceived and gave birth to three sons and two daughters. And the boy Samuel grew before the LORD."

My prayer for you is that you will see children as God's gift to your family as well as to the world. God wants to use us to influence our generation from the bottom up, not the top down. As we disciple both our physical and our spiritual children, we will have an impact in our homes, our congregations, and our society and will bring honor to the name of the Lord.

QUESTIONS FOR REFLECTION AND DISCUSSION

1. What are the desires of your heart?

2. Are you praying that God will give you a husband who loves the Lord?

3. Are you praying that God will bring back a husband who has strayed from the Lord?

4. Maybe you are struggling with a health issue.

5. Maybe you are bitter and angry about a circumstance in which you find yourself.

6. Perhaps it's an issue of injustice; perhaps it's not injustice toward you but toward your husband or your children.

7. Are you grieving because of a shattered dream, a miscarriage, the death of a loved one, a fruitless job, a loveless marriage, or rebellious children?

Charm is deceitful and beauty is vain,
but a woman who fears the Lord,
she shall be praised

Proverbs 31:30

אֵשֶׁת־חַיִל

Chapter 5

BEING IN YOUR RIGHT MIND

THE ISSUE OF SENSIBILITY

*"To be sensible, pure, workers at home, kind,
being subject to their own husbands, so that the word of God
will not be dishonored."*
Titus 2:5

Before we take a deeper look at the third issue or quality of being sensible, let's review the order of the list from Titus 2:3-5. Because this third quality of being sensible (v. 5) or in your right mind, fits into the theme of Titus chapter 2, I first intended to begin with sensibility, but I soon realized that the order of the words has a purpose.

As a result of this Divine order, we began with *husband-lovers*: we learned that marriage is God's invention, and we are to respect the idea of having a husband. God has designed man and woman to become one flesh.

This union reflects and foreshadows His intimate love for Israel and the congregation of Messiah.

From this overview of marriage, we went to *children-lovers* and saw that children are indeed a blessing from the Lord and are the foundation and future of our society. God builds and influences His world through children, like Samuel, the great leader of his day who anointed King David. Ultimately, the Messiah Himself chose to come into this world as a baby.

We noted that, regardless of our marital status, we should respect and pray for marriages. These two broad issues are the foundation for our homes and our communities.

These next two issues, "*to be sensible*" and "*pure*," are meant to help us understand how God's teaching in this passage works in a practical way. If we can understand that our lives as women are to be founded on being "husband-lovers" and "children-lovers," then these next two qualities, "sensible" and "pure" can give us the practical tools we need to grow spiritually.

The quality "*to be sensible*" comes from the Greek word *sophron* and means being in your right mind, to be of sound mind, or prudent. It can also mean to be self-controlled or temperate.

Some of you might be thinking:

"Listen, I'm divorced. I tried that marriage stuff, and it didn't work."

"My marriage isn't working. Even though I look like I'm happily married, I refuse to respect my husband and this marriage. I'm just going to live my life and make the best of a bad situation."

"My kids are grown, and I have "done my part"

"I am not planning on getting married or having kids so what in the world does this teaching have to do with me?"

If any of these objections mirror yours, please keep reading. It is my fervent prayer that there are answers for you here.

What does it mean for a person to be sensible? Synonyms of sensible will give us a clearer picture. *Sensible* includes the ideas of being sober, wise, reasonable, and having or showing good sense or judgment. Being sensible also implies a reliable ability to reach intelligent conclusions, that is, to judge and decide with soundness and prudence. It means having good judgment that has been tempered and refined by experience, training, and maturity.

We must understand who we are in the Lord, otherwise life will not make sense! In order to better understand this concept of being sensible or in our right minds, let's look at examples in the Scriptures where this same word is used. The first example is in Romans 12:3, and it has to do with esteem where Paul gives us a way to see ourselves as God sees us.

> Romans 12:3—For through the grace given to me I say to every man among you not to think more highly of himself than he ought to think; but to think so as to have *sound judgment,* as God has allotted to each a measure of faith.

The words "sound judgment" is the same word for *sensible* or being in your right mind.

What Is Self-Esteem?

Self-esteem is your perception of yourself. I recently watched Geena Davis being interviewed on a popular news show. She is forty-nine years old and portraying the President of the United States in a new TV series, "Commander and Chief." The reporter asked her why she began to model, which then led her into acting. She replied that while growing up she had low self-esteem and said, "If millions of people will see me and love me, then I think that I will feel better about myself." However, she quickly added, "I was wrong; it didn't help! I think that many actors go into the acting business because of low self-esteem issues."

Maybe some of you can relate. I know I can. If I am living apart from God's intention for my life, it should not be surprising that I would still struggle with low self-esteem, inadequacy, and even depression. In contrast, if I base my self-esteem and personal value on God's Word, then I have the self-confidence to understand who I am as His child.

How do you determine your self-image? Are you determining your self-esteem according to the world's values or according to God's? Romans 12:3 says that you should not think too highly of yourself. This is pride and arrogance. Implied in this phrase is the idea of not thinking too lowly of yourself, either, which would lead to inferiority or low self-esteem. In either case, pride or inferiority, the focus is on one's self. To have sound judgment and see ourselves as God sees us, we must by faith, through the grace of God, find our significance in our Creator.

We should never doubt our worth in the eyes of God. It must remain in our mind that as His children we are "in Messiah," and to be so guarantees us a position in His family. Colossians 2:9 and 10 says that you are complete in Messiah because He has made you complete. "For in Him all the fullness of Deity dwells in bodily form, and in Him you have been made complete, and He is the head over all rule and authority."

When the Lord looks at you, He sees you clothed with the garments of salvation and wrapped in His righteousness. This is the hottest fashion ticket in town! But do you see yourself covered in His salvation and standing in His righteousness? Notice what is said in Isaiah

> Isaiah 61:10 —I will rejoice greatly in the LORD, my soul will exult in my God; for He has clothed me with garments of salvation, He has wrapped me with a robe of righteousness, as a bridegroom decks himself with a garland, and as a bride adorns herself with her jewels.

In the context of Paul exhorting the believers at Rome to have sound judgment about who they are, he also exhorts them to present themselves as a living and holy sacrifice, which is only reasonable in light of what the Lord has done for them. He also warns them to not be conformed to this world, but to be transformed by the renewing of their minds (Romans 12:1-2). These verses confirm that when we are sensible, which is the product of the "renewing of the mind," we likewise will be confident.

We are called to holiness, which means that we must set aside worldly issues and concentrate on heavenly issues.

In the Hebrew Scriptures, one could only enter into the presence of the Holy God through sacrifices and the high priest. But now *we* are the temple of the Holy God. You and I! Do we reflect God's holiness in our lives? Are we living in light of and preparing our temple for eternity?

In a recent interview with a reporter, Rick Warren of *The Purpose-Driven Life* fame said,

> People ask me, what is the purpose of life? And I respond. In a nutshell, life is preparation for eternity. We were made to last forever, and God wants us to be with Him in Heaven. One day my heart is going to stop, and that will be the end of my body—but not the end of me. I may live sixty to one hundred years on earth, but I am going to spend trillions of years in eternity. This is the warm-up act, the dress rehearsal. God wants us to practice on earth what we will do forever in eternity. We were made by God and for God, and until you figure that out, life isn't going to make sense.

I agree with Rick. I want to live in preparation for eternity and glorify the Lord with my life through *my* holy temple. This is how I will find my true esteem in Him.

Being In Your Right Mind ~Mentally

The word *sensible* is also used for being in your right mind mentally or being in your right mind about life. In Mark, we find a demon-possessed man who was so out of control that he could tear apart and break off shackles and chains when others tried to subdue him.

This demon-possessed man was like the living dead as he roamed among the tombs and graveyards, cutting himself with stones as the demons controlled him.

But when Yeshua came, He cast out the Legion and sent the demons into the swine. What happened to this man after he met the Messiah Yeshua, Son of the Most High God? His life was radically changed as he went from darkness to light. Here the word for *sensible* is used to describe the once demon-possessed man as now being *"in his right mind."*

> Mark 5:15—And they came to Yeshua and observed the man who had been demon-possessed sitting down, clothed and in *his right mind*, the very man who had the "legion"; and they became frightened.

That's what the Messiah can do for us as well. Maybe our circumstances are not as extreme as a demon - possessed man, but if we are without faith in the Lord or live carnally apart from Him, then we cannot really be in our right minds.

Do you sometimes watch the news and shake your head thinking, "How can people be so crazy and violent, taking guns into our schools and randomly killing?"

How can we mentally be in our right minds, showing good judgment and discernment? We need to let God control us and acknowledge our total dependency on the Lord. Without His control, we have no constraints over our emotions, our wants, and our desires. In 2 Corinthians, Paul exhorts us to take "every thought captive to the obedience of Messiah."

2 Corinthians 10:3-5—For though we walk in the flesh, we do not war according to the flesh, for the weapons of our warfare are not of the flesh, but divinely powerful for the destruction of fortresses. We are destroying speculations and every lofty thing raised up against the knowledge of God, and we are taking every thought captive to the obedience of Messiah.

Do you allow the Lord to dominate your thought life? Do you take every thought captive to the obedience of Messiah?

WORDS OF SOBER TRUTH

In the book of Acts, Paul is asked to defend himself before Festus and his distinguished visitor, King Agrippa. Paul was being held in Caesarea, and the Jewish leadership wanted him to go up to Jerusalem to stand trial for charges brought against him. But in Acts 25:3, it says that these same men were setting an ambush to kill Paul.

As a Roman citizen, Paul appealed to Caesar. Before he was sent to Rome, however, King Agrippa (grandson of Herod) and Bernice visited Caesarea to pay their respects to Festus. Paul was summoned to be tried before these dignitaries. In Acts 26, Paul gave a dramatic account of his testimony, including how the Lord had appeared to him on the road to Damascus. Toward the end of Paul's defense, Festus interrupted in a loud voice:

Acts 26:24-25—Paul, you are out of your mind! Your great learning is driving you mad. But Paul said, I am not out of my mind, most excellent Festus, but I utter words of *sober* truth.

This word *sober* is based on the same Greek word that means sensible (*sophron*) or to have soundness of mind. Festus was accusing Paul of being crazy, when in fact Paul was the one who understood the truth of God's Word and the purpose for His creation. How encouraging this testimony should be for us who share our faith and are misunderstood and falsely accused. We need to understand that our faith in Messiah Yeshua is the *Truth* that will put us in our right minds and also give us God's perspective about ourselves and others.

Consider the opposite of having a sound mind or being in your right mind: unstable, immodest, indiscreet, unwise and crazy are just a few examples of the person lacking sensibility. We need to consider whether any of these traits describe our actions.

LIKE A CITY WITHOUT WALLS

The word picture in Proverbs 25:28 describes an unstable person.

Proverbs 25:28 —Like a city that is broken into and without walls is a man who has no control over his spirit.

Walls gave protection and security to the city, so this proverb says that when we lack sound judgment or sensibility, we open ourselves up to the enemy and danger from every side. Before modern weapons, most ancient cities relied upon high, thick walls for a defense. The Great Wall of China was built to keep out invaders, yet of the several times it was breached, none of them were because of the wall being broken down; all were the result of betrayers within.

He who has no control over his own spirit, whether because of pride, lust, anger, or whatever, has a betrayer within to overthrow the city of his soul. "Prayerful, watchful self-control is the wall of the city, and we should see to it that there is no breach made in it by self-reliance or spiritual indolence" (Faussett).

Many a man has destroyed himself, after others had failed to have much influence over him to destroy him. In truth, man is often his own worst enemy.

Being In Your Right Mind - Physically

This word picture leads us into our next use of the word "sensible," which has to do with how to be in your right mind about your clothing and appearance. 1 Timothy 2:9 says, "I want women to adorn themselves with proper clothing modestly and *discreetly*." Why do we dress the way we do? Some women use their clothing, (or lack of it), to try to bait men. Some of us think that if we look good physically, flaunting it adds to our self esteem. But the Scriptures exhort us to be modest and to be in our right minds (*sensible*) when it comes to how we dress.

We need to teach younger women to please the Lord in all aspects of their lives including how they dress.

BEAUTY WITHOUT DISCRETION

Another word picture in Proverbs 11:22 gives us one description of a woman who lacks sensibility or sound judgment, "As a ring of gold in a swine's snout, so is a beautiful woman who lacks discretion."

A jewel cannot do anything for a pig; for all of its washing, it still prefers the mud.

If a woman, no matter how beautiful, has no sense of right and wrong, her very beauty will ultimately be a snare to her. True beauty is not an outward fairness but an inward graciousness.

Kenneth Boa, in his book *Conformed to His Image*, writes encouraging words for all of us about our self image as he asks the question, "*Who Defines You?*"

We are constantly in danger of letting the world instead of God define us, because that is so easy to do. It is only natural to shape our self-image by the attitudes and opinions of our parents, our peer groups, and our society. None of us are immune to the distorting effects of performance-based acceptance, and we can falsely conclude that we are worthless or that we must try to earn God's acceptance. Only when we define ourselves by the truths of the Word rather than the thinking and experiences of the world can we discover our deepest identity.

The Scriptures exhort us to look to Messiah, not to self, for the solutions we so greatly need. I have come to define the biblical view of self-love in this way: loving ourselves correctly means seeing ourselves as God sees us. This will never happen automatically, because the scriptural vision of human depravity and dignity is countercultural.

To genuinely believe and embrace the reality of who we have become as a result of our faith in Messiah requires consistent discipline and exposure to the Word of God. It also requires the context of fellowship and encouragement in a community of like-minded believers. Without these, the visible will overcome the invisible, and our understanding of this truth will gradually slip through our fingers.

What does it mean to see ourselves as God sees us? Contrary to culture, the biblical doctrine of grace humbles us without degrading us and elevates us without inflating us. It tells us that apart from Messiah, we have nothing and can do nothing of eternal value. Our past has been changed because of our new heredity in Messiah, and our future is secure, because of our new destiny as members of his body.

Grace teaches us that the most important thing about us is not what we do, but whose we are in Messiah. In Scripture, doing (our actions), should flow out of being (our identity): the better we grasp our identity in Messiah the more our actions should reflect His character.

In other words, think about who you are in Messiah before you act! It is critical that *sensibility* becomes a habitual part of your life. What a help it is when the pressures of life fall upon you, and you find that you possess the ability to have God's sense about them.

Being In Your Right Mind –Spiritually

The final area of being sensible or in our right minds is found in the book of 2 Timothy.

2 Timothy 1:7 –For God has not given us the spirit of fear but of power and love and a *sound mind*.

Fear can be good! Fear is used in both the Hebrew Scriptures and the New Covenant in several significant ways. The first kind of fear is found in both the Old and New Covenants. In Hebrew it is denoted by the word *yirah*, and in Greek it is *phobos*. Both of these words speak of an awesome respect for the majesty and holiness of God.

King David speaks of this *fear* as clean and pure (Psalm 19:9). Gentiles who wanted to follow and trust the God of Israel or convert to Judaism were called God-fearers (Acts 10:2, 22). Both Solomon and the Psalmist declare that this kind of *fear* is the beginning of wisdom.

> Proverbs 1:7 – The *fear* of the Lord is the beginning of wisdom: fools despise wisdom and instruction.

Another kind of fear (*deilia* in the Greek) is cowardice or timidity. It is found in 1 Timothy 1:7, where Paul was writing to Timothy who was a young leader dealing with all kinds of problems. He needed encouragement, and Paul wrote, "for God has not given us the spirit of fear but of power and love and a *sound mind.*"

This same word for *fear* is used by Messiah on several occasions. When Messiah's disciples needed His assurance, He told them that He would send the Holy Spirit to be their Helper, and He would give them His shalom, His peace. In light of this, Messiah says to them:

> John 14:27 — Peace I leave with you; My peace I give to you; not as the world gives, do I give to you. Let not your heart be troubled, nor let it be *fearful.*

> Matthew 8:26 — And Messiah said to the disciples when he calmed the raging storm, "Why are you *timid,* you men of little faith?" Then He arose, and rebuked the winds and the sea; and it became perfectly calm.

Are there "storms" in your life that are making you afraid or cowardly? What or who do you fear? What makes you nervous and afraid?

In Psalm 56:3-4 it says, "*When* I am afraid, I will put my trust in Thee, in God, whose word I praise, in God I have put my trust; I shall not be afraid."

The word "when" in Hebrew is *yom* and means in the day, whenever, or while. For David, it was not a matter of *if* he would be afraid but *when* he would be afraid.

David was writing this in the midst of trials; he was being taken captive by the Philistines in Gath. His enemies were after him. He knew that in a time of trouble, or as the Hebrew puts it, "in the day" I am afraid or "when" I am afraid, he would put his trust in the Lord.

It is a blessed fear which drives us to trust the Lord. Our fear can turn to faith and reverence for a Holy God as we declare, "in God, whose word I praise, in God I have put my trust" (Psalm 56:4). As a child of God, what is the worst thing that could happen to you? David poignantly says in Psalm 56

> Psalm 56:9-11—Then my enemies will turn back in the day when I call; this I know, that God is for me. In God, whose word I praise, in the LORD, whose word I praise, in God I have put my trust, I shall not be afraid. What can man do to me?

Indeed, what can mere men do to you if you are a child of God? Instead of being timid or a coward — having the spirit of fear— God wants you to have His spirit of power (*dunamis*) and to be in your right mind (*sophronismo*).

Ken Boa's book, *Conformed to His image*, includes a list that gives us much to think about. I've included a small portion of the list that answers the question: *Who does God say I am?*

- *I am a child of God*: John 1:12—"But as many as received Him, to them He gave the right to become children of God, even to those who believe in His name."

- *I am a branch of the true vine, and a conduit of Messiah's life*: John 15:1, 5—"I am the true vine, and My Father is the vinedresser...I am the vine, you are the branches; he who abides in Me, and I in him, he bears much fruit; for apart from Me you can do nothing."

- *I am a friend of Messiah*: John 15:15—"No longer do I call you slaves, for the slave does not know what his master is doing; but I have called you friends, for all things that I have heard from My Father I have made known to you."

- *I have been justified and redeemed*: Romans 3:24—"Being justified as a gift by His grace through the redemption which is in Messiah Yeshua."

- *My old self was crucified with Messiah, and I am no longer a slave to sin*: Romans 6:6—"Knowing this, that our old self was crucified with Him, that our body of sin might be done away with, that we should no longer be slaves to sin."

- *I will not be condemned by God*: Romans 8:1—"There is therefore now no condemnation for those who are in Messiah Yeshua."

- *My body is the temple of the Holy Spirit, who dwells in me*: 1 Corinthians 3:16—"Do you not know that you are a temple of God, and that the Spirit of God dwells in you?"

- *I have been made complete in Messiah*: Colossians 2:10—"In Him you have been made complete and He is the head over all rule and authority."

Thought Questions

1. How do you determine your esteem, your value?

2. What does it mean to take every thought captive, under the control of Messiah?

3. How does our dress reflect what is in our hearts?

4. What or whom do you fear?

5. How do you deal with your fears?

6. How do you measure your beauty?

*Strength and dignity are her clothing,
and she smiles at the future*

Proverbs 31:25

אֵשֶׁת־חַיִל

Chapter 6

ABIGAIL

A WOMAN WITH REAL SEKHEL

We have discussed the four areas of being sensible and now have a foundational understanding of what it means to be in one's right mind. The first basic truth is *sound judgment*, which is related to having proper self-esteem and is confirmed by Romans 12:3. The second aspect of being *sensible* includes being in a your **right** mind and responding in *sober* truth, which are substantiated by Mark 5:15 and Acts 26:25. The third aspect is that we are to dress *discreetly*, and is validated by 1 Timothy 2:9. Finally, we learned how we are to see ourselves spiritually, which was verified by 2 Timothy 1:7.

If we women can understand our self-esteem, our self-image, our mental health, and our spiritual walk as God intends, then we have a chance to be in our right **minds** and have a positive impact for the Lord on our **families** and communities, even in the midst of very difficult circumstances.

Remember how Hannah was able to pour out all her bitterness and disappointment to the Lord, even when constantly taunted by her rival Peninnah? Another woman in Scripture is also an outstanding model of "sense and sensibility." Her name is Abigail, which in Hebrew means "My father is Joy." Abigail's name is derived from two Hebrew words: *Avi*—my father and *gayeel*—joy.

Setting The Stage

Before we look at the account of Abigail in 1 Samuel 25, we need to set the stage by understanding what transpired in the previous chapter. In 1 Samuel 24, we find Saul still pursuing David and seeking his destruction, "Saul took three thousand chosen men from all Israel, and went to seek David and his men (v. 2) Saul went into a cave to relieve himself (v. 3)." **Saul failed to realize that in the** inner **region** of the cave, **David and his six hundred men** were hiding.

David's men **thought that this was a perfect** opportunity for David to destroy Saul. However, David did not agree. Instead, he chose to cut off the edge of Saul's robe, but even this relatively benign act bothered his sensitive conscience.

Samuel 24:5-6—And it came about afterward that David's *conscience* bothered him because he had cut off the edge of Saul's robe. So he (David) said to his men, "Far be it from me **because** of the LORD that I should do this thing to **my lord,** the LORD's anointed, to stretch out my hand **against** him, since he is the LORD's anointed."

The word for conscience is the Hebrew word *lev*, which means heart, inner man, will, or understanding.

David had a heart that was sensitive to the Lord, so he declared that he would not do anything against the Lord's anointed.

The rest of the chapter tells us of David confronting Saul to let him know that he had not killed him when he had the opportunity. David did not take matters into his own hands but was determined to wait on the Lord. This must have been a testimony of patience and constraint to his men, for David had sacrificed the opportunity to rid himself of his arch enemy.

Scripture records Saul's response to David:

> 1 Samuel 24:17-18—And he (Saul) said to David, "You are more righteous than I; for you have dealt well with me, while I have dealt wickedly with you. And you have declared today that you have done good to me, that the LORD delivered me into your hand and yet you did not kill me."

David's restraint became a testimony not only to David's six hundred men, but also to Saul and his three thousand men. It was a loud and clear statement that David was a servant of God who waited on Him for his deliverance and vindication as the future King of Israel. What a victory for David!

Practical Wisdom Exemplified

In the next chapter, which tells the story of Abigail and her husband Nabal, it seems as though David went from a great victory almost to the agony of defeat. Abigail is described in verse 3:

> 1 Samuel 25:3—Now the man's name was Nabal, and his wife's name was Abigail. And the woman was *intelligent* and *beautiful* in appearance, but the man was harsh and evil in his dealings, and he was a Calebite.

The two English words *intelligent* and *beautiful* are interesting phrases in Hebrew. Intelligent is actually two Hebrew words: *tovat sekhel*; *tovat* means "good" and *sekhel* means "understanding." *Sekhel* is a common Yiddish word that means good sense, judgment, or common sense. When someone does something wise or discerning, it could be said: "She has real sekhel!" A person can be intelligent but not necessarily display good judgment or common sense.

Let's examine a few other uses of *sekhel*. David used this word when he gave the charge to Solomon to build the Temple of the Lord in 1 Chronicles 22:12, "Only the LORD give you *discretion* and understanding, and give you charge over Israel, so that you may keep the law of the LORD your God." Solomon also used *sekhel*, in Proverbs 19:11, "A man's *discretion* makes him slow to anger, and it is his glory to overlook a transgression."

The use of *sekhel* in these examples helps us understand that Abigail was not merely smart. She was discerning and knew how to use her intelligence.

Abigail was also "beautiful in appearance." In the Hebrew this is "beautiful in form:" *yafat tohar*. The first word, *yafat*, means "beautiful" and the second word, *tohar*, means form or appearance. Other uses of *tohar* or "form" can be found in Genesis 29:17 where Rachel is said to be fair of form (*tohar*).

In 1 Samuel 16:18, the teenage David is described: "Then one of the young men answered and said, 'Behold, I have seen a son of Jesse the Bethlehemite who is a skillful musician, a mighty man of valor, a warrior, one prudent in speech, and a *handsome* (*tohar*) man; and the LORD is with him.'"

Look at this list! Among his other wonderful attributes, David is described as handsome. Like David, Abigail was not "just another pretty face" with a shapely body. She was a skilled woman who understood and practiced sound judgment and sensibility.

I believe that Abigail's beauty was not just skin deep; she had an inner radiance and appearance that was under the control of an intelligent and discerning mind.

The Black Sheep Of The Family

In contrast, Abigail's husband Nabal is described as harsh, (*kasha* in the Hebrew). This word *kasha* is used in Exodus 33:5:

> For the LORD had said to Moses, "Say to the sons of Israel, you are an *obstinate* people; should I go up in your midst for one moment, I would destroy you. Now therefore, put off your ornaments from you, that I may know what I will do with you."

And again in Exodus 6:9...

> So Moses spoke thus to the sons of Israel, but they did not listen to Moses on account of their despondency and *cruel* bondage.

The cruel, obstinate character of Nabal led to actions that are described as evil, *raah*. This word *raah* is a very common word for evil.

One example is found in Genesis 6:5 where it is used twice for wickedness and evil, "Then the LORD saw that the *wickedness* of man was great on the earth, and that every intent of the thoughts of his heart was only *evil* continually."

1 Samuel 25:3 also tells us that Nabal was a Calebite, which means that he came from the line of Caleb.

Remember Caleb? He was the spy who, along with Joshua, believed God's promise that the children of Israel would be able to enter the Promised Land.

> Numbers 32:12—Except Caleb the son of Jephunneh the Kenizzite and Joshua the son of Nun, for they have followed the LORD fully.

Caleb and Joshua were the only two who believed God and His promises as they were on the brink of entering Canaan. But this godly heritage from Caleb did not seem to rub off on Nabal. Rather, Nabal was an arrogant person whose deeds were evil.

In the next section of 1 Samuel, we read of a request from David's men to Nabal.

> 1 Samuel 25:4-8—David heard in the wilderness that Nabal was shearing his sheep. So David sent ten young men, and David said to the young men, "Go up to Carmel, visit Nabal and greet him in my name; and thus you shall say, 'Have a long life, peace be to you, and peace be to your house, and peace be to all that you have.'

And now I have heard that you have shearers; now your shepherds have been with us and we have not insulted them, nor have they missed anything all the days they were in Carmel. Ask your young men and they will tell you. Therefore let my young men find favor in your eyes, for we have come on a festive day. Please give whatever you find at hand to your servants and to your son David."

This all seems reasonable enough. Nabal was a wealthy Israeli sheep herder, and this was sheep shearing time—a time of celebration when there was extra food on hand. The request was not unreasonable, because David's men had protected Nabal's sheep herders in previous months.

But Nabal's response, found in verses 10 and 11, was not just impolite; it was rude and abrasive, heaping one insult on top of another.

1 Samuel 25:10-11—When David's young men came, they spoke to Nabal according to all these words in David's name; then they waited. But Nabal answered David's servants, and said, "Who is David? And who is the son of Jesse? There are many servants today who are each breaking away from his master. Shall I then take my bread and my water and my meat that I have slaughtered for my shearers, and give it to men whose origin I do not know?"

Take a closer look at verse 11, and count how many times Nabal says "I" and "my." There are at least seven occurrences! Compare this attitude of Nabal with the "rich man" in Luke 12:13-21. Both of these men were fools who failed to acknowledge that God is the source of all blessing and provision. They were fools who met with similar ends.

Luke 12:16-21—And He (Yeshua) told them a parable, saying, "The land of a rich man was very productive. And he began reasoning to himself, saying, ` What shall *I* do, since *I* have no place to store *my* crops?' Then he said, `This is what *I* will do: *I* will tear down *my* barns and build larger ones, and there *I* will store all *my* grain and my goods. 'And *I* will say to my soul, '*Soul, you* have many goods laid up for many years to come; take *your* ease, eat, drink and be merry.' But God said to him, 'You fool! This very night your soul is required of you; and now who will own what you have prepared?' So is the man who stores up treasure for himself, and is not rich toward God."

Nabal not only failed to recognize that his provision comes from the Lord, he also failed to acknowledge David as the anointed future king of Israel. Nabal is the poster child of the fool from the parable.

Nabal's Cup Of Insults Overflows

Of course the "breaking away from his master" comment in 1 Samuel 25:10 is a direct reference to Saul. Nabal knew full well who David and his men were but chose to insult them nevertheless. He did not recognize David as God's anointed, the future King of Israel.

When David's men came back and reported this to David, he responded in verse 13. David said to his men, "Each of you gird on his sword. So each man girded on his sword. And David also girded on his sword, and about four hundred men went up behind David while two hundred stayed with the baggage" (1 Samuel 25:13).

We see in verses 21 and 22 what David intended to do:

1 Samuel 24:21-22—Now David had said, "Surely in vain I have guarded all that this man has in the wilderness, so that nothing was missed of all that belonged to him; and he has returned me evil for good. May God do so to the enemies of David, and more also, if by morning I leave as much as one male of any who belong to him."

What an overreaction! Have you ever wondered how men of God who walk with the Lord and do amazing things for Him sometimes make stupid, rash mistakes? In *The Life of David* A. W. Pink says:

The "mature believer" is not the one who has learned to walk alone but he who most feels his need of leaning harder upon the everlasting arms. He knows that in his flesh dwells no good thing and that only from Messiah can his fruit be found. Left to one's self the wisest believer does not have any better judgment that the young believer.

In the previous chapter, David had a huge victory. He could have killed his enemy, but because of Saul's position as King, David did not harm him. He trusted the Lord and was an outstanding leader and example to his men. David kept his anger under control and avoided the temptation of revenge against Saul, whose jealous desire was to kill him.

David did not expect such reproachful language and insolent treatment from Nabal. David was insulted, his pride was hurt, and suddenly he was out for revenge. He forgot that "Vengeance is mine, says the Lord, I will repay" (Romans 12:19). David forgot who he was in the Lord.

Instead of remembering that God was in control and seeking Him, David let his hurt feelings dictate his response. Why would David decide to take matters into his own hands over such an insignificant incident?

LITTLE FOXES THAT RUIN THE VINE

Sometimes little things cause us to lose our testimony. The Shulamite woman in the Song of Solomon understood this. She did not want anything, like a small doubt concerning her lover's faithfulness, to spoil their blossoming love.

She therefore declared, "Catch the foxes for us, the little foxes that are ruining the vineyards, while our vineyards are in blossom" (Song of Solomon 2:15).

The little foxes could ruin the vine by cunning and stealth. The fox was also a picture of false teaching of the prophets of Israel (Ezekiel 13:3).

Cunning behavior and false teaching might not seem like a "big deal" at first, but these "little foxes" had to be caught before they ruined the vineyard of their blossoming love. This incident with Nabal was a "little fox" that could have spoiled the vine, and it almost ruined David's reputation.

I can identify with both David and the Shulamite woman. In my life, it is usually not the big problems that cause me to stumble and lean on my own understanding. When a catastrophic event takes place, whether a sudden illness of a family member or an obvious attack from the evil one, I know I cannot face the difficulty without depending totally on the Lord. So I immediately seek the Lord and His strength as my first resource.

Often the seemingly insignificant decisions or relationship problems that arise in my life are the ones in which I neglect to seek the Lord. Instead, I attempt to muddle through the problem using my own finite intellectual prowess.

When I take matters into my own hands and do not seek the Lord, a little sin can lead to bigger ones.

We need to keep in mind Hebrews 12:15, "See to it that no one comes short of the grace of God; that no root of bitterness springing up causes trouble, and by it many be defiled." We must not allow a seemingly small irritation to grow into a life threatening cancer.

Let us take a closer look at how this could have happened to David. In 1 Samuel 25:1, we **gain some insight**:

> 1 Samuel 25:1—Then **Samuel died; and** all Israel gathered together and mourned for him, and buried him at his house in Ramah. And David arose and went down to the **wilderness of** Paran.

A smaller temptation is likely to prevail after a greater one has been resisted. Due to David's exile and his flight from the tyranny of Saul, he had probably been unable to mourn with his people when Samuel died. This may have left him more vulnerable and less conscious of his need for God's delivering grace.

When his **men came** back to him with Nabal's rejection, he could have "**cast his** care on the Lord" (Psalm 55:22), **We are** admonished in Proverbs 3:5-6 to trust the Lord **in all his** ways. David forgot his calling, and his hurt pride **manifes**ted itself.

Into this scene, with an insulting fool as a husband one side and David out for revenge on the other, enters Abigail. Her servant, who must have realized that their lives were in danger, came to warn Abigail.

> 1 Samuel 25:14-19 –But one of the young men told Abigail, Nabal's wife, saying, "Behold, David sent messengers from the wilderness to greet our master, and he scorned them. Yet the men were very good to us, and we were not insulted, nor did we miss anything as long as we went about with them, while **we were** in the fields. They were a wall to us both by **night and** by day, all the time we were with them tending the sheep. Now therefore, know and consider what you should do, for **evil is plotted against our master and against all** his household; and he is such a worthless man that no one can speak to him." Then Abigail hurried and took two hundred loaves of bread and two jugs of wine and five sheep already prepared and five measures of roasted grain and **a hundred clusters of raisins and** two hundred cakes of figs, and loaded them on donkeys. And she said to her young men, "Go on before me; behold, I am coming after you." But she did not tell her husband Nabal.

Abigail understood the dire situation and acted immediately. Why didn't she tell her husband? She was in emergency mode. The lives of her husband and her entire household were at stake. She needed God's wisdom and discernment to determine her course of action. In verse 18, it says that she hurried and, with the help of her household staff who trusted and respected her, prepared an enormous amount of food to take to David.

ABIGAIL'S APPROACH TO DAVID

1 Samuel 25:23-24 says, "When Abigail saw David, she hurried and dismounted from her donkey, and fell on her face before David, and bowed herself to the ground. And she fell at his feet and said, 'On me alone, my lord, be the blame. And please let your maidservant speak to you, and listen to the words of your maidservant.'" Notice in verse 23 that she fell on her face and bowed to the ground. This Hebrew word for bow actually means to "prostrate oneself." This word is used to describe the priests in the Temple when they worship the Lord. Picture this scene: this beautiful woman is before David, falling on her face - lying flat before him - showing respect and humility. In verse 24 her position is reiterated: "she fell at his feet," and in her prostrated state, made an incredible apology.

1 Samuel 25:25—Please do not let my lord pay attention to this worthless man, Nabal, for as his name is, so is he. Nabal is his name and folly is with him; but I your maidservant did not see the young men of my lord whom you sent.

Abigail took the blame upon herself and, by doing so, redirected David's anger from Nabal to herself. This is a wonderful example of the proverb "A soft answer turns away wrath" (Proverbs 15:1). What amazes me and speaks to me of how I want my actions to influence others is that she continued to minister to David in verses 26-31. She did not keep the focus on herself, which may have been easy for David to accept because of her beautiful, humble, and gracious appearance.

Abigail diverted David's focus from Nabal, to the Lord and to God's calling and promises for his life.

> 1 Samuel 25:26-31—Now therefore, my lord, as the LORD lives, and as your soul lives, since the LORD has restrained you from shedding blood, and from avenging yourself by your own hand, now then let your enemies, and those who seek evil against my lord, be as Nabal. And now let this gift which your maidservant has brought to my lord be given to the young men who accompany my lord. Please forgive the transgression of your maidservant; for the LORD will certainly make for my lord an enduring house, because my lord is fighting the battles of the LORD, and evil shall not be found in you all your days. And should anyone rise up to pursue you and to seek your life, then the life of my lord shall be bound in the bundle of the living with the LORD your God; but the lives of your enemies He will sling out as from the hollow of a sling. And it shall come about when the LORD shall do for my lord according to all the good that He has spoken concerning you, and shall appoint you ruler over Israel, that this will not cause grief or a troubled heart to my lord, both by having shed blood without cause and by my lord having avenged himself. When the LORD shall deal well with my lord, then remember your maidservant.

To say these profound truths and give such a great perspective of David's life, Abigail must have been inspired by the Spirit of God. Abigail's words in verse 26 reminded David that "the Lord has restrained you from shedding blood, and from avenging yourself by your own hand." Had she heard of David's restraint in the cave with Saul and how Saul had responded?

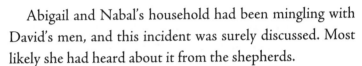

Abigail and Nabal's household had been mingling with David's men, and this incident was surely discussed. Most likely she had heard about it from the shepherds.

It should also be noted that Abigail displayed humility and wisdom that only the grace of God could have given her. Many might think that she was a cunning woman who used her beauty and the empty stomachs of David and his men to gain the upper hand and save her position as Nabal's wife. Such is not the case. She was an instrument of the Holy God who brought a man after God's own heart to a rational state of mind. We must always keep in mind that losing control of our emotions can lead to sin and embarrassment before the congregation of God.

DAVID'S RESPONSE TO ABIGAIL'S EXHORTATION

1 Samuel 25:32-35—Then David said to Abigail, "Blessed be the LORD God of Israel, who sent you this day to meet me, and blessed be your discernment, and blessed be you, who have kept me this day from bloodshed, and from avenging myself by my own hand. Nevertheless, as the LORD God of Israel lives, who has restrained me from harming you, unless you had come quickly to meet me, surely there would not have been left to Nabal until the morning light as much as one male." So David received from her hand what she had brought him, and he said to her, "Go up to your house in peace. See, I have listened to you and granted your request."

Abigail had bowed before David and spoken from her heart, a heart that truly reflected the promises and purposes of God for David. Then he responded to her.

David first blessed the Lord God of Israel, whom he acknowledges to have sent Abigail as God's messenger. In other words, David saw that she represented His God, and he was thankful.

He praised Abigail for her discernment, discretion, and sound judgment. As a result of her unselfish actions, David was restrained from taking vengeance and having the blood of innocent people on his hands. He graciously received the gift of food and encouraged Abigail to return to her home in peace, or shalom.

As Abigail returned to her home, she must have been asking God for wisdom to communicate all that had taken place to her husband. Upon returning to her house, she saw that a feast was taking place, and Nabal was very drunk. So she waited until the next morning, when Nabal had a chance to become sober.

> 1 Samuel 25:37-38—But it came about in the morning, when the wine had gone out of Nabal, that his wife told him these things, and his heart died within him so that he became as a stone. And about ten days later, it happened that the LORD struck Nabal, and he died.

In His time, God dealt with Nabal and his foolish, arrogant actions against God's anointed. When the news of Nabal's demise reached David, he said: "Blessed be the LORD, who has pleaded the cause of my reproach from the hand of Nabal, and has kept back His servant from evil. The LORD has also returned the evildoing of Nabal on his own head." Then David sent a proposal to Abigail to take her as his wife (1 Samuel 25:39).

Indeed, the Lord blessed Abigail, and in time she became David's wife. Because this study of Abigail is intended to demonstrate that she showed *sense* or *good judgment*, it will be helpful to review the four areas of sensibility in relation to the life of Abigail.

First, how did she view herself (self perception)? She saw herself as a servant of the Most High God. She was not defined by her husband's terrible reputation or character. What her husband said about her or how he treated her did not define who she was. She was presented with a difficult situation, but by the grace of God and her undying trust in Him, she was able to be of sound mind and see herself as a daughter of the God of Israel.

Secondly, how was her state of mind (mental stability)? When the crisis came, she did not panic. She did not break down and become paralyzed with fear; rather she "cast her care on the Lord" and used discernment and good judgment in putting a plan together.

Thirdly, how did others view her (her appearance)? We have already noted that she was beautiful, but her beauty was more than skin deep. Her loveliness was part of her character that gave her the trust and respect of those around her (her servant who confided in her, members of her household who helped her prepare and traveled with her, and David, who responded to her request).

Fourthly, how was her spiritual life? Abigail did not have a spirit of timidity. She displayed God's power and love and her own sound mind as she pointed David to the Lord and to His plan and promises for David's life.

Abigail's actions were rooted in her trust in what the Lord could do. She was confident that David was the Lord's anointed and should be honored.

She could see that her husband's foolish response could bring death to her entire household and be a shameful reproach on David as well. She was able to take the blame upon herself. In a sense, she said, "Take my life instead of those of my husband and my family."

God used her to diffuse the situation, bring peace, and help David to be the man of God he desired to be.

I pray that we would all seek to be in our right minds — to be sensible so that we can live for the Lord and honor Him with our lives. And speaking of honoring God with our lives, get ready for the next chapter, because God wants to purify you!

You may be reading this book and enjoying certain aspects of the teaching, but if you have not yet come to trust in the Messiah and depend on His provision and atonement, you will not be able to connect fully with this material. I can almost hear someone saying, "This sounds too ideal. I can't respect my husband, and I have no desire to have children. Hey, I'm pretty smart, and I'm certainly in my right mind about most things."

I understand that these qualities are ideal. It is God's Word and His holy standard that I am presenting. Until you have personal faith in who the Messiah is and what He has provided for you, an intimate relationship with the Living God will elude you, and this book may be more frustrating than helpful. I would urge you to place your faith in Yeshua by simple trust and become the daughter of the King. Then continue reading and enjoy!

THOUGHT QUESTIONS

1. If Abigail had not used sound judgment but had panicked, what do you think the outcome would have been?

2. If David had gone through with his plan to murder every male in Nabal's household, what kind of testimony would this have been to his men? To all of Israel? To his kingship?

3. Have you ever overreacted in an **unscrip**tural way to a situation that was seemingly ins**ignifica**nt? Have you ever done so right after a spiritual **victory**?

4. What can we learn from Abigail who, like Hannah, was in a very difficult home situation?

An excellent wife, who can find?
For her worth is far above jewels

Proverbs 31:10

Chapter 7

The Issue of Purity

According to God's Design

Do you like to decorate your home? Change the furnishings or the color of the walls? Maybe you are a professional interior decorator!

Many women have a wonderful gift for decorating their homes, and their decorations reflect their tastes, likes and dislikes. In this chapter, we will look at how God wants His holy temple decorated.

God's holy dwelling reflects His nature. Because He is sinless and pure, we, His temple, need to understand and strive for purity so that we can reveal God's preferences in His furnishings.

In the Old Covenant, the Hebrew word for pure, *tahor*, is used fifty-eight times, mostly in Exodus and Leviticus, to describe the furnishings and utensils of the Tabernacle. The majority of the references use pure to describe the gold.

The mercy seat and the lampstand or *menorah* are just two examples:

> Exodus 25:17 –And you shall make a mercy seat of gold (*tahor*), two and a half cubits long and one and a half cubits wide.

> Exodus 25:31 –Then you shall make a lampstand of pure gold (*tahor*). The lampstand and its base and its shaft are to be made of hammered work; its cups, its bulbs and its flowers shall be of one piece with it.

During Israel's history, God related to them as a people through worship in the Tabernacle and eventually the Temple. God's presence, or *shekinah* - glory, dwelt in His Tabernacle. Just as these furnishings reflected the character and holiness of God Himself, so God wants our lives — the temples of the living God — to reflect His holiness and His purity. Thus, it is of vital importance to understand His purifying process in our lives.

As we are called to purity, we are likewise called to conform to the image of Messiah. Therefore, it is essential for older women to teach younger women the characteristics found in Titus 2:3-5 as the final phrase in our text reiterates:

> Titus 2:3-5—Older women likewise are to be reverent in their behavior, not malicious gossips, nor enslaved to much wine, teaching what is good, that they may encourage the young women to be husband-lovers, to be children-lovers, to be sensible, *pure*, workers at home, kind, being subject to their own husbands, *that the word of God may not be dishonored.*

In the previous chapters, we noted that the third quality of being in your right mind, or sensible, has to do with your self image, your mental health, your outward demeanor, and finally, your spiritual walk. As we seek the mind of the Lord in all of these areas, we develop sound judgment and live a life honoring to the Lord.

The quality of being "pure" or "chaste" is essential for our daily walk and our growth in the Lord. Part of developing and obtaining sound judgment is to realize that God is purifying us through testing and the difficulties of life. The purifying process enables us to grow stronger and allows us to draw closer to Him. We need to understand how God wants to use trials and tribulations to help us develop a more intimate walk with Him. As someone wisely said, "We want our problems to make us better, not bitter."

This word *pure* or *chaste* in the Greek is *hagnos* and means free from ceremonial defilement, holy, sacred, free from sin, or innocent. The Hebrew word *tahor* (pure) conveys the same idea as does the Greek word. The English dictionary gives us some additional insight into the meaning of *pure* and *chaste*. It defines pure as "spotless, stainless, and free from moral fault or guilt, and unmixed with any other matter as in pure gold."

Let us consider several ways in which this word *pure* (*hagnos*) is used in the New Covenant. As Paul was speaking to the congregation at Corinth, he used the word pure to reflect a *moral loyalty*, as to a spouse.

2 Corinthians 11:2-3—For I am jealous for you with a godly jealousy; for I betrothed you to one husband, that to Messiah I might present you as a *pure* virgin. But I am afraid, lest as the serpent deceived Eve by his craftiness, your minds should be led astray from the simplicity and *purity* of devotion to Messiah.

Just as any man would be jealous if his wife "played the harlot" and went after other men, so Messiah is jealous, wanting you to be pure and faithful to Him alone and not to prostitute yourself to the gods of this world. You are His pure virgin. He has cleansed you and bought you with His blood. But we can be very creative in our desire and ability to go after other men, ideas, teachers, or thoughts that will take us away from the purity of the Lord.

How Was Eve Led Astray?

She was led astray by the craftiness of the evil one. Paul writes, "lest your minds should be led astray from the simplicity and *purity* of devotion to Messiah."

Eve's curiosity and her insatiable desire to be like God led her to listen to Satan, the father of lies. Paul was concerned about the Corinthians. He reminded them of Eve's experience and warned them not to be deceived as Eve was.

The word *mind* can also be translated "purpose" or "thought". The seeds of doubt that the serpent sowed refocused Eve's thoughts, away from the pure relationship she had with her Creator. Her deception began as she listened to the serpent and began to think, "Maybe God has not given me everything that I need; maybe God is holding back on me."

Throughout the chapter, Paul warns the Corinthians not to be taken in by false teachers and apostles. As he defends his position and authority as a true apostle, he warns them.

2 Corinthians 11:13-14—For such men are false apostles, deceitful workers, disguising themselves as apostles of Messiah. And no wonder, for even Satan disguises himself as an angel of light.

Is your thought life leading you towards purity or defilement? You might be saying in your heart, "What I think is my business! It's not hurting anyone, and besides, I'm the only one who is aware of it!" Or you might say, "I can think about another man. It's nothing more than an innocent flirtation."

It all begins in the mind

Others enjoy a fantasy thought life based on personal desires of being thinner, smarter, prettier, or richer. When you are mentally distracted, you are an open season for Satan "who disguises himself as an angel of light."

Walter Mitty is a *fictional character* in James Thurber's short story *The Secret Life of Walter Mitty*, published in 1941. Mitty is a meek, mild man with a vivid fantasy life. In a few dozen paragraphs, he imagines himself a wartime pilot, an emergency-room surgeon, and a devil-may-care killer. What a sad epitaph - that a person's entire life is lived in a world of his own making. This is a pathetic attempt to escape the reality and responsibility of life. So it is with the believer who escapes to a world of his or her own making, declining a pure relationship with the Lord for the secret desires of the heart.

A closer look at Genesis proves that Eve hoped that the forbidden fruit would make her wise.

> Genesis 3:6—When the woman saw that the tree was good for food, and that it was a delight to the eyes, and that the tree was desirable to make one *wise*, she took from its fruit and ate; and she gave also to her husband with her, and he ate.

It was interesting for me to discover that this word "wise" used in Genesis 3:6 is a verb form of the same word used to describe Abigail in 1 Samuel 25. We saw that Abigail was described as a woman of good understanding — intelligence, or *sekhel* in Hebrew.

This intelligence meant that she was not only smart but also able to discern and exercise wisdom, or function in her right mind in matters pertaining to herself. Abigail had *sekhel* or wisdom based on a comprehension of God's values. The word parallels the issue that we previously studied: to be in your right mind, of sound mind, self-controlled, or sensible (*sophron*).

Even though Eve lived in Paradise, her desire for wisdom opened her up to temptation. Paul was concerned that, like Eve, the believers in Corinth would go after the false teachers and false apostles of the day, thereby opening themselves up to deception that would lead them away from the purity of their devotion to Messiah.

Paul's call to purity must have been difficult for the believers in Corinth who came from an immoral and impure society. It may have been especially difficult for the believing women of Corinth to understand the value of purity, when impurity was the order of the day.

Yet what ground has been gained by contemporary society? Paul's call to the Corinthians echoes loudly in today's self-indulgent and sin-loving society.

Light That Pierces Through The Darkness

In the book *The Measure of a Woman* Gene Getz writes:

> In the city of Corinth more than one thousand women served as priestesses in the Temple of Aphrodite. After the gospel penetrated this licentious city, Paul wrote to the Corinthian believers, outlining a spectrum of immoral activities that characterized these people before they came to faith in Messiah.

Paul is stirring up the believers in Corinth by way of reminder of what Messiah has accomplished in them.

> 1 Corinthians 6: 9-11—Or do you not know that the unrighteous shall not inherit the kingdom of God? Do not be deceived; neither fornicators, nor idolaters, nor adulterers, nor effeminate, nor homosexuals, nor thieves, nor the covetous, nor drunkards, nor revilers, nor swindlers, shall inherit the kingdom of God. And such were some of you; but you were washed, but you were sanctified, but you were justified in the name of the Lord Yeshua the Messiah, and in the Spirit of our God.

Those who have been delivered from great darkness should desire to live in the light. When we understand that purity begins in our thought life, we can go to the second aspect of purity found in the New Covenant: purity is the initial quality of godly wisdom.

Wisdom from above vs. widsom from below

> James 3:17-18—But the wisdom from above is first pure, then peaceable, gentle, reasonable, full of mercy and good fruits, unwavering, without hypocrisy. And the seed whose fruit is righteousness is sown in peace by those who make peace.

Remember that Eve wanted the fruit to make her wise. James 3:14-18 not only tells us how to recognize godly wisdom, but also gives us a list to help identify worldly, demonic wisdom:

> James 3:14-16—But if you have bitter jealousy and selfish ambition in your heart, do not be arrogant and so lie against the truth. This wisdom is not that which comes down from above, but is earthly, natural, demonic. For where jealousy and selfish ambition exist, there is disorder and every evil thing.

Where there is jealousy, where there is a heart motivated by selfish ambition or arrogance, there you will find lying, deceit, and treachery. The wisdom that is generated from envy, selfishness, and pride is based on the flesh, the world, and the devil. Eve's wisdom turned out to be selfish ambition, and in her arrogance she thought she knew better than her Creator.

Many times I make a decision about a seemingly mundane matter, forgetting to consult the Lord and ask for His guidance, leaning on my own understanding. Eve must have reasoned, "After all, it's just a piece of fruit in a beautiful garden. What could the harm be in having a bite?"

What We Say Matters

The preceding verses (James 3:14-16) teach us the characteristics of pure wisdom. The "tongue," or what we say, can be used for great good or great destruction. The purity of our devotion to Messiah and the kind of wisdom we have, whether worldly or heavenly, is evident in our communication with one another. Because we are the verbal gender, it is of utmost importance that our speech be under the control of the Holy Spirit.

The book of James gives us an overview of the tongue and how it relates to those who desire to mature.

James 3:1—Let not many of you become teachers, my brethren, knowing that as such we shall incur a stricter judgment.

Because teachers use the tongue as an instrument of communication and instruction, they have a greater potential for misusing words. Therefore, James cautions would-be teachers to make certain that their gift of teaching is indeed from the Lord. Teachers have not only been given the gift of teaching, they have also inherited the great responsibility of using sound judgment for the content of their teaching and will be judged accordingly.

The Power Of Words

James 3:2 says that "we all stumble in many ways." This stumbling, which refers to an obstacle causing someone to strike his foot and fall, happens to everybody, including teachers. We all make mistakes and have moral lapses.

If this were not true, we would not be human. But verse 2 goes on to say that "If anyone does not stumble in what he says, he is a perfect man, able to bridle the whole body as well."

The idea of the "perfect man" does not mean sinlessness. It describes a person who is progressing toward spiritual maturity and is able to bridle the tongue, thereby controlling his speech. Again it does not mean that this person will never stumble, but the life of the spiritually mature teacher should be characterized by a decline in verbal mistakes. Self-control is the process of reigning in one's speech.

James now gives two examples of the power of the tongue. Both illustrate that something small can control something bigger.

> James 3:3-4—Now if we put the bits into the horses' mouths so that they may obey us, we direct their entire body as well. Behold the ships also, though they are so great and are driven by strong winds, are still directed by a very small rudder, wherever the inclination of the pilot desires.

The first example is the bridle in a horse's mouth and the second example is a ship's rudder. The purpose of a horses' bridle is that "they may obey us" and the result is that the whole body can be "turned around" or change direction. Ships are driven by an outside force - "strong winds"- while horses are possessed with a will of their own that needs to be curbed.

What strength our tongue has! James goes on to picture how this small body part can cause such great destruction.

James 3:5-12—So also the tongue is a small part of the body, and yet it boasts of great things. Behold, how great a forest is set aflame by such a small fire! And the tongue is a fire, the very world of iniquity; the tongue is set among our members as that which defiles the entire body, and sets on fire the course of our life, and is set on fire by hell. For every species of beasts and birds, of reptiles and creatures of the sea, is tamed, and has been tamed by the human race. But no one can tame the tongue; it is a restless evil and full of deadly poison. With it we bless our Lord and Father; and with it we curse men, who have been made in the likeness of God; from the same mouth come both blessing and cursing. My brethren, these things ought not to be this way. Does a fountain send out from the same opening both fresh and bitter water? Can a fig tree, my brethren, produce olives, or a vine produce figs? Neither can salt water produce fresh.

Both the potential destruction that comes from our own sinful nature and that which comes from outside problems (which can bring hurricane force winds) can be controlled by a tongue that is yielded to the Lord.

Is it your desire to be a teacher of the Word? Do you want to grow in spiritual maturity? If you answer yes to either of these questions, you must understand that the focus of life will be witnessed in your speech.

Our Blessed Hope

Purity is the hallmark of the woman who walks with God. Another practical way to keep ourselves pure is to fix our hope on the return of our Messiah, Yeshua. This fixation is our "blessed hope," and the idea of hope is an expectation or a sure fact.

> 1 John 3:2-3—Beloved, now we are children of God, and it has not appeared as yet what we shall be. We know that, when He appears, we shall be like Him, because we shall see Him just as He is. And everyone who has this hope fixed on Him *purifies* himself, just as He is *pure*.

If we understand that our hope and expectation for this life are to be lived in the light of the Messiah's appearing, we will desire to live pure lives.

King David sought purity. In Psalm 51:10, he prays, "Create in me a clean (*pure*) heart O God." This is the prayer of my heart as well. But how does God purify us? When we trust in Messiah's atonement, our sins are forgiven. However, we still sin everyday and need His forgiveness and cleansing! The book of 1 John describes Messiah's daily purification work:

> 1 John 1:7-10—But if we walk in the light as He Himself is in the light, we have fellowship with one another, and the blood of Yeshua His Son cleanses us from all sin. If we say that we have no sin, we are deceiving ourselves, and the truth is not in us. If we confess our sins, He is faithful and righteous to forgive us our sins and to cleanse us from all unrighteousness. If we say that we have not sinned, we make Him a liar, and His word is not in us.

The Struggle Of The Flesh

Given that the book of I John is written to believers, we realize that even after coming to faith, we will struggle with our sin nature throughout our lives.

If we say we do not have this sin nature any longer, we are not only self-deceived, we do not even have the truth in us. Verse 10 tells me that as a believer I will commit sin, and if I deny this fact, I make God a liar and do not understand His Word.

As a new believer in high school, I lived a carnal life. On the one hand, I desired to grow in the Lord, while at the same time I thought that such growth would mean that I would have to break off a relationship with my unsaved boyfriend which I was not ready to do.

I remember talking with a mature believer who had been instrumental in helping me find the Lord. He was not only mature in the Lord, but he was also in college, so as a high school student I respected him and his knowledge of the Word. He told me that my struggle was not unusual, and then we read a portion from Romans 7:14-25 where the struggle of the flesh and the new man is pictured. I exclaimed, "This **is exa**ctly what I feel like."

I knew that **even though** my sins were forgiven for eternity, the need for **daily** purity was a tremendous challenge. Understanding and memorizing 1 John 1:9 helped me to see my sinful nature which can only be understood through a biblical perspective. Verse 9 gives a conditional promise: If I confess my sins, then Messiah Yeshua is faithful and righteous to not only forgive me but cleanse me.

Calling Sin By Its Worst Name

When the Greek word says confess, (*homologeo*) it means "to speak the same," or, in other words, to agree with God about our sin. It took me years of growth in the Lord to understand how grievous sin is to the heart of God.

In our culture today, we use euphemisms to rationalize our sins. A euphemism is a nicer sounding word to replace a harsh reality. We tend to lighten up our sin when God wants us to confess it and bring it down to its worst name.

One example that hits home for me is my rebellion. It may have to do with a request from my husband, or from my employer, or a task I need to accomplish, but my flesh says: "I am tired and I just don't want to do it," or "This is not appealing to me, and I refuse to obey." In the book of 1 Samuel, we see what rebellion is to God.

> 1 Samuel 15:23a—For rebellion is as the sin of witchcraft, and stubbornness is as iniquity and idolatry.

These words were spoken by the prophet Samuel to King Saul and give us a clear picture of what rebellion is like before God. When I think of how my sin of rebellion is as "the sin of witchcraft" to God, it takes me to a deeper level of contrition and the realization that I need His cleansing, not just daily but constantly. Rebellion is my rejection of God's will.

This is just one example of our many euphemisms for sin. The attitude of "everyone else has one" is called covetousness, and in Colossians it is called for what it really is: idolatry.

Colossians 3:5—Therefore consider the members of your earthly body as dead to fornication, uncleanness, passion, evil desire, and *covetousness, which is idolatry.*

God wants us to bring everything down to its worst name because that is what He died for. Therefore, it is imperative that we see sin for what it is and realize how odious it is before a Holy God.

As C.H. Spurgeon said, "Our Messiah did not die for imaginary sins, but His heart's blood was spilt to wash out deep crimson stains, which nothing else can remove." Isaiah 1:18 says, "'Come now, and let us reason together,' says the LORD, 'Though your sins are as scarlet, they will be as white as snow; though they are red like crimson, they will be like wool.'"

As Gold Refined

How does God reveal these sins in our lives? One illustration that helps me to understand this process is the "refiner's pot."

Nelson's Book of Illustrations vividly describes the process of refining gold by the goldsmith:

One day, missionary Amy Carmichael, who devoted her life to rescuing girls who had been dedicated to a life of slavery and shame in Indian Hindu Temples, took some of her children to see a goldsmith refining gold, in the ancient manner of the Orient. The man sat beside a small charcoal fire. On top of the coals lay a common, red, curved roof-tile, and another tile lay over it like a lid. This was his homemade crucible. The man had a mixture of salt, tamarind fruit, and burnt brick dust, which he called his "medicine" for the purifying of the gold. He dropped a lump of ore into the blistering mixture and let the fire "eat it." After awhile, the man lifted the gold out with a pair of tongs, let it cool, and studied it. Then he replaced the gold in the crucible and blew the fire hotter than it was before. This process went on and on, the fire growing hotter and hotter. "[The gold] could not bear it so hot at first," explained the goldsmith, "but it can bear it now; what would have destroyed it helped it." As the children watched the gold being purified in the fire, someone asked the man, "How do you know when the gold is purified?" The man answered, "When I can see my face in it [the liquid gold in the crucible], then it is pure." When the Great Refiner sees his own image reflected in us, He has brought us to purity and maturity.

Comparing this illustration to our lives, let us examine how the purification process works. The process begins with the impure gold, which can represent our lives. Positionally, we are pure before the Lord, still possessing a carnal nature, and having it until we are in glory with Him.

We need to understand that, even as believers, this carnal nature is there as we go through the problems of life. 1 John 1:8 says, "If we say that we have no sin, we are deceiving ourselves, and the truth is not in us."

The gold in the pot over intense heat represents us as we go through disappointments and catastrophes that God allows to come into our lives. The intense heat is necessary in order to bring the dross to the top, so that it can be removed. 1 Corinthians 10:11-13 gives us a greater understanding as to why God brings testing or the heat of purification into our lives.

Temptation Or Testing?

1 Corinthians 10:11-13—Now these things happened to them as an example and they were written for our instruction, upon whom the ends of the ages have come. Therefore let him who thinks he stands take heed lest he fall. No temptation has overtaken you but such as is common to man; and God is faithful, who will not allow you to be tempted beyond what you are able, but with the temptation will provide the way of escape also, that you may be able to endure it.

From this passage we learn that problems and trials are part of life, and even the struggles of others can serve as an example to encourage us. For when it says temptation, it also means testing.

First of all, we see that testing is common to everyone. No one is exempt from the trials of this life. Messiah told his disciples, "These things I have spoken to you, that in Me you may have peace. In the world you have tribulation, but take courage; I have overcome the world" (John 16:33).

Secondly, the Scriptures assure us that God is in control. Because we know that God is good, the things that He permits to happen in our lives flow out of His goodness. He is also faithful and knows how to work all things together for our ultimate good. It is so encouraging for me to realize that God knows me and will not allow me to be tested beyond my ability to endure, and that He will keep me and bring me through the testing. The Lord gives the victory because He is with us through the trial.

He also assures us that He will provide a way of escape. What is that way? Messiah taught His disciples a way of escape in Matthew 26:41, "Keep watching and praying that you may not enter into temptation; the spirit is willing, but the flesh is weak."

Prayer is the way of escape. When we persevere in our trials by depending on His strength, we bring glory to His name and show our love for Him. As James describes in 1:13, "Blessed is a man who perseveres under trial; for once he has been approved, he will receive the crown of life which the Lord has promised to those who love Him."

A Shocking Discovery

The dross is our response to problems: anger, bitterness, envy, jealousy, etc. We should not be too surprised to see what comes from our hearts when the heat of trials become more intense.

Messiah, who saw what is inside the heart, pointed out, "For from within, out of the heart of men, proceed the evil thoughts, fornications, thefts, murders, adulteries, deeds of coveting and wickedness, as well as deceit, sensuality, envy, slander, pride and foolishness. All these evil things proceed from within and defile the man" (Mark 7:21-23).

When the fires of testing or trials take place in our lives, impurity and sin are revealed. For instance, when I was single and lived in a tiny New York City apartment, I liked to walk around in my bare feet. Sometimes I would stub my toe, thereby producing profuse pain. Then an unsolicited curse word would involuntarily come out of my mouth.

My first response was to be embarrassed and look around, hoping no one heard me. Then I would wonder, "Where did that come from? That's not what I'm really like is it? It's that throbbing toe that made me say those words." My tendency would be to deny the cursing and bury it as if it had never occurred. (I can be very creative in blaming my circumstances or others for my sin.) But as I've matured in my faith, I've learned to quickly confess the sin to the Lord and ask for his forgiveness.

You might be thinking that this "toe stubbing incident" seems like such a little thing — a few expletives when you feel intense pain. But this example is but one of many that show me what I'm really like without the control of the Holy Spirit. I have these potentially evil responses ready to come out of my carnal self.

C.S. Lewis put it this way, "If you turn a flashlight on and you see the rats, it's not the flashlight that created the rats, the light just exposed what was already there."

When the evil or sin surfaces, we need to confess it, agree with God that it is sin, and be cleansed by the power of Messiah's atonement.

Our Heavenly Goldsmith

The goldsmith removes the dross as it floats to the top — that is the Lord Himself, our Heavenly Goldsmith, who will remove the dross or sin as we confess it. However, we must first identify the dross in our lives. Yes, He knows what is in our hearts, and He provided the cure, the cleansing element and the permanent solution by taking all that dross, all that sin, and washing it with His own blood. We need to acknowledge our sinfulness and our need for Him moment by moment, then with humility receive His forgiveness and righteousness.

Even when we are sinful, He remains faithful not only to forgive but also to forget. This idea of forgiving our sins and remembering them no more is found in a passage in Micah 7:19 where it says, "He will again have compassion on us; He will tread our iniquities under foot. Yes, Thou wilt cast all their sins into the depths of the sea." Indeed, He makes us pure.

Purity is the result of the transformation from dross into pure gold. The same kind of transformation takes place as we are being conformed to the image of Messiah. When we submit to that process, we enjoy restored intimacy with our God. Maturity is the process by which we trust solely in the Lord, as we walk with Him daily. We have nothing to fear because God shows us the condition of our heart through His testing. As King David prayed to the Lord, "Examine me, O LORD, and try me; Test my mind and my heart," (Psalm 26:2).

How we respond to the trials we experience reveals what we depend on. Do we depend on the flesh, or on God's grace? For we are His pure virgin bride. As such, we should love His appearing and purify ourselves, even as He is pure.

Let's pray that we will grow in purity so that we will not dishonor the Word of God. As the dross is removed and the reflection of His purity shows forth in our lives, we will mature in our walk with Him and in our daily conduct.

We should identify with what Paul wrote in 2 Corinthians 3:18: "But we all, with unveiled face beholding as in a mirror the glory of the Lord, are being transformed into the same image from glory to glory, just as from the Lord, the Spirit."

Can you imagine if in our educational system there were never any tests of any kind? How would the teachers measure the learning and growth of the students? The only way you can know if there is learning is through testing. In the school of life, God brings us through various trials. He loves us with an everlasting love, and He desires to have an intimate relationship with us day by day. So do not fear the testing and the trials that will come. Rather, welcome them as His tool to keep you always depending on His grace, His goodness, and His plan for you.

THOUGHT QUESTIONS

1. Read Romans 7:14-25. Does this describe your struggle?

2. According to this passage in Romans, where can we find victory in our struggles?

3. Are you growing in the area of controlling your speech?

4. Are you going through testing right now?

5. Are there areas of your thought life that you need to confess to the Lord?

6. Do you love His appearing, and are you living in view of Yeshua's return?

7. Can you identify a euphemism of sin in your life?

A Woman of Valor looks well to the ways of her household, and does not eat the bread of idleness

Proverbs 31:27

Chapter 8

WORKERS AT HOME

THE DOMESTIC DIVA

Older women ... may encourage the young
women to be ...workers at home.
(Titus 2:3-5)

"Workers at Home." I do not know about you but this phrase does not appeal to me. I enjoyed discussing God's view of marriage and children, and the idea of being in my right mind appeals to me. Even the purifying process of becoming more like Messiah is something I can appreciate and strive for. But now we come to the practical phrase, "workers at home." I was the fourth of five children and, according to Dr. Kevin Leman in his book *The Birth Order Book*, the fourth born leaves home as soon as possible, never to return. Dr. Leman was certainly right in my case.

I left my hometown to attend college and then moved to New York City after graduating.

I know the idea of home is supposed to bring warm, fuzzy feelings, like the Hallmark commercials that air around the holidays, but when I was younger, I would rather be traveling, ministering, eating out with friends and stopping by my home just to refuel.

In the past few lessons, we studied how to be sensible and pure. Both of these issues have to do with the inward quality of our lives. Sensibility pertains to how we view ourselves, our thought life, our mental health, and finally our spiritual life. When we discussed purity, we saw that God wants to refine us like pure gold, to bring honor to Him as He transforms us into His likeness.

The next three qualities – *"workers at home," "good,"* and *"subject to your own husband"* - are practical out-workings of being in our right minds and the need for the Lord's purifying process. That process is crucial if we are to live out these last three qualities.

When Sam and I had our first son, I began to understand the importance of home life. Creating a loving home with God's values as its basis became my goal, and I believe that's what this phrase is saying.

"Workers at home" is made up of two Greek words. *Oikos*, which refers to a house or dwelling that includes the people and the place, and *ergon* which means "to do work" and refers to specific deeds. Messiah Yeshua told his disciples in John 4:34, "My food is to do the will of Him who sent Me, and to accomplish His *work*." The word "work" is *ergon*, the same Greek word found in our phrase "workers at home."

So if we take the example of Messiah as He lived his life to complete, perfect, or reach the goal that God had given Him, we can begin to understand what this phrase says to us women. Just as Yeshua gave Himself to His work, so we are to fulfill and accomplish our roles as homemakers, and be devoted to home duties.

Within the culture of the women that Paul was writing to, this phrase was probably not unfamiliar. After all, the women of the first century did not just bake from scratch: they harvested and winnowed the wheat, then ground the flour!

Of course, the care and nursing of children were also part and parcel of a woman's life. According to the *Mishna*, ancient Jewish writings, "If any women worked apart from their husbands in the marketplace or at a trade, they were considered a disgrace. A wife could, however, work at crafts or horticulture in the home and sell the fruits of her labor."

But the Jewish laws were clear: the woman's priority was in the home. She was to take care of all the needs of her home, her children, her husband, strangers, the poor and needy, and guests. The wife who faithfully discharged her responsibilities was held in high regard in her family, in the synagogue, and in the community.

Is it any surprise that today's culture takes a dim view of stay-at-home mothers? To a generation raised to believe in the absolute equality of the sexes, the sacrifices and accommodations that women continue to make in marriage seem arbitrary and unfair.

In marriages in which both husband and wife work, why should women still do more of the household chores? Why do we assume that it will be the mother, and not the father, who will curtail her ambitions for the sake of the children?

I remember when our first son Joshua was born. We lived in an apartment in New York City, and I had a friend who offered to baby sit so that I could go back to work part-time in the ministry. So when Joshua was three months old, I left him crying with my friend and went to catch a subway to our office, which was located downtown by Grand Central Station. I decided to buy a cup of coffee and a muffin on the way. While sitting in my office, I could not get Josh out of my mind, but I rationalized that it was only part-time and that I would be back home in several hours. It took me a few days to realize that Josh was my ministry. If I could do some things from home, that would be great, but if I were to leave home to work, even bringing in a little extra money was a myth, because with subway fare, paying my friend the sitter (and don't forget my coffee and muffin), I would only break even financially. I think that this was the beginning of understanding not only that the Lord wanted me home, but also that my child was now my primary ministry. This was the high calling for my life: to be a wife, a mother, and a worker at home.

There is no virtue in staying at home unless we have God's perspective on it. We need to understand how He desires us to be a homemaker or a worker at home. The book of Proverbs sheds light on this subject. It distinguishes between a woman who is a builder and one who is a destroyer.

Proverbs 14:1—The wise woman builds (*banah*) her house, but the foolish tears it down with her own hands.

In the children-lovers lesson, we discussed the word *build* from Psalm 127:1 where it says, "Unless the LORD builds the house, they labor in vain who build it; unless the LORD guards the city, the watchman keeps awake in vain."

In Proverbs 14:1, the same Hebrew word is used for "to build" (*banah*), and we learned that the Hebrew word for house (*bayit*), son and daughter are all based on the root "to build."

Are You Building Or Destroying?

Are you a woman who uses the wisdom given to her by God and seeks His grace to build her home? Or does the second phrase more aptly describe your home? Sometimes I see myself being foolish and tearing down my home with my own hands. This Hebrew word *haras* means tear down, overthrow, destroy, ruin. It implies total destruction!

How can we destroy our homes with our own hands? As I look at the meanings of this word *haras* or "tear down," one idea comes strongly to my mind. If I am rebelling against God and looking to my flesh to guide me, the results will be ruinous for my life and my home. My response to problems at home can be anger or manipulation, instead of love and ministry. I may chose to complain, responding like the contentious woman in Proverbs 21:9, which says, "It is better to live in a corner of a roof, than in a house shared with a contentious woman."

A contentious woman causes strife and discord. This is not the way to build up our homes. Psalm 11:3 says, "If the foundations are destroyed (*haras*), what can the righteous do?"

We need to build our lives and our homes upon the solid foundation of the principles found in God's Word in order to understand God's view of marriage and children. Each of us needs to ask herself, "Do I respect and love what He has given me? Am I a wise woman who will minister through my home?"

Who Is That Noble Woman?

The excellent woman described in Proverbs 31 knows how to build up her home. Proverbs 31 was written by King Lemuel's mother. Lemuel means "toward God" or "devoted to God," but there is no information about this King. Some commentators think that Lemuel could be another name for Solomon and therefore, this passage was written by Bathsheba.

> One wonders in concert with Jewish tradition if King Lemuel's mother might not have been Bathsheba who orally passed the family heritage of Ruth's spotless reputation along to David's son Solomon. Lemuel could have been a family name for Solomon (see Jedediah, 2 Samuel 12:25), who then could have penned Proverbs 31:10-31 with Ruth in mind. (MacArthur, J. *Women of Faith, Bravery and Hope*).

Suffice it to say that this noble woman loved her son and discipled him to understand that, in light of his calling as a King, he needed to marry a woman of valor.

Do you find Proverbs 31 intimidating or exhilarating? I have always found it to be an unwelcome challenge.

Who is this woman who gets up so early, runs a business from her home, makes all the clothes by hand (no Singer sewing machine) and never seems to have a negative thing said about her? Like me, you might be thinking, "I'm not married to a king, and I don't have any servants." But if you are a believer in Messiah, you are a child of the King of Kings, adopted into the royal family with all the privileges and responsibilities that go with the calling. The resources available to you are infinite. You are a daughter of the King, with all the potential to be a woman of valor.

DESCRIPTION OF A WORTHY WOMAN

Let's consider Proverbs 31 in light of a woman who epitomized the phrase, "worker at home" by comparing her to Ruth. Solomon was only a few generations removed from Ruth's son, Obed, so it is reasonable to think that Ruth was one of the models for this passage.

Think of a woman who has had a positive impact on you. Was it a godly mother, grandmother, or great aunt?

In the original language, Proverbs 31:10-31 takes us through the twenty two letters of the Hebrew alphabet (*alef-beit*) as it begins with *Alef* and then each verse begins with the next letter of the alphabet. This portion takes us through the *Alef-Beit* or ABC's of being a woman of valor.

Proverbs 31:10-31 – An excellent wife, who can find? For her worth is far above jewels. The heart of her husband trusts in her, and he will have no lack of gain. She does him good and not evil all the days of her life.

She looks for wool and flax and works with her hands in delight. She is like merchant ships; she brings her food from afar. She rises also while it is still night and gives food to her household and portions to her maidens. She considers a field and buys it; from her earnings she plants a vineyard. She girds herself with strength and makes her arms strong. She senses that her gain is good; her lamp does not go out at night. She stretches out her hands to the distaff, and her hands grasp the spindle. She extends her hand to the poor, and she stretches out her hands to the needy. She is not afraid of the snow for her household, for all her household are clothed with scarlet. She makes coverings for herself; her clothing is fine linen and purple. Her husband is known in the gates, when he sits among the elders of the land. She makes linen garments and sells them, and supplies belts to the tradesmen. Strength and dignity are her clothing, and she smiles at the future. She opens her mouth in wisdom, and the teaching of kindness is on her tongue. She looks well to the ways of her household, and does not eat the bread of idleness. Her children rise up and bless her; her husband also, and he praises her, saying: "Many daughters have done nobly, but you excel them all." Charm is deceitful and beauty is vain, but a woman who fears the LORD, she shall be praised. Give her the product of her hands, and let her works praise her in the gates.

Proverbs 31:10 says, "An excellent wife, (*eshet chayil*), who can find? For her worth is far above jewels."

The word *eshet* can mean wife, female, or woman. In this context, "wife" is clearly fitting, but I trust that whatever your position in life, you will find this passage meaningful.

Verse 10 asks a rhetorical question. The writer is letting us know that this *"woman of valor"* is rare.

The next word *hayil* is translated "excellence" or "valor." The word is used 230 times in the Hebrew Scriptures and, depending on the context, can mean courage, wealth, bravery, resolute, determined, or strength.

Our Proverbs 31 woman and Ruth are women in Scripture to whom the word *hayil* is applied.

In Ruth 3:11, Boaz calls Ruth a woman of valor. The same phrase *"eshet hayil"* is used: "And now, my daughter, do not fear. I will do for you whatever you ask, for all my people in the city know that you are a *woman of excellence* (valor)." Boaz makes this declaration before they are officially married and before she gives up her gleaning job.

Ruth ~ A Woman Of Excellence

Is Ruth really a woman of valor? When we meet her, she is returning to Israel from Moab with her bitter mother-in-law, Naomi. When the women of Bethlehem see Naomi in Ruth 1:19, they ask, "Is this Naomi?" It is not difficult to discern Naomi's state of mind when she replies, "Do not call me Naomi; call me Mara, for the Almighty has dealt very bitterly with me. I went out full, but the LORD has brought me back empty. Why do you call me Naomi, since the LORD has witnessed against me and the Almighty has afflicted me?" (Ruth 1:20-21).

Here we have Ruth the Moabite with a bitter, desperately poor mother-in-law who does not even acknowledge her to the women of Bethlehem.

Naomi did not realize that God would use Ruth to bring her back to her senses and show her His love and provision. Instead, Naomi accused God of bringing evil upon her and stripping her of everything.

The *Proverbs 31* woman engenders loyalty and trust from her family and community.

> Proverbs 31:11-12, 23—The heart of her husband trusts in her, And he will have no lack of gain. She does him good and not evil all the days of her life. Her husband is known in the gates, when he sits among the elders of the land.

Such loyalty and trust can only result from her relationship with the Lord. But how does this apply to Ruth, who is not yet married and does not have a home of her own? Many of us are familiar with Ruth's amazing declaration of loyalty and allegiance to Naomi and the God of Israel:

> Ruth 1:16-17—But Ruth said, "Do not urge me to leave you or turn back from following you; for where you go, I will go, and where you lodge, I will lodge. Your people shall be my people, and your God, my God. "Where you die, I will die, and there I will be buried. Thus may the LORD do to me, and worse, if anything but death parts you and me."

She chooses not to return to the home of her father (the pagan land of Moab) but rather to follow Naomi, her people, and her God. When Ruth made this promise, she had no idea what lay ahead. How could she be so strong? It took great valor to face an unknown country and what would seem to be a life of poverty.

Finding Strength In The Lord

Ruth 1:18 gives a clue as to where Ruth gets her courage: "When she (Naomi) saw that she (Ruth) was *determined* to go with her, she said no more to her."

Naomi saw that Ruth was determined. The word "determined" is *ametz* in the Hebrew and carries the idea that *she strengthened herself*. The same word is used in the phrase "Be strong and of *good courage*" where God encourages Moses and Joshua in their leadership roles (Deuteronomy 31:6, 7, 23; Joshua 1:6, 7, 9, 18). Likewise, Isaiah 41:10 says, "I will *strengthen* you."

As Ruth turns to the God of Israel and declares that He is her God, He gives her courage and strength.

We find the same root word in Proverbs 31:17: "She girds herself with strength, and makes her arms *strong*." The *Proverbs 31* woman did not work in her own strength and courage. Rather, she trusted the Lord to make her strong and capable.

Ruth, our woman of valor, found determination and courage in the Lord and ministered to Naomi, whose heart was broken and weighed down with grief.

WHATEVER IT TAKES TO BUILD UP THE HOME

For me, one of the most intimidating things about the *Proverbs 31* woman is how hard she works to build up her home. She is a whirlwind of activity and develops her abilities in the process. Verses 13-16 contain just some of the examples of her work ethic:

❧ Proverbs 31:13 —She looks (seek with care) for wool and flax, and works with her hands in delight.

Wool is for the colder season and flax is used to make linen for the warmer weather, so she prepared for all kinds of weather.

❧ Proverbs 31:14 —She is like merchant ships; she brings her food from afar.

This woman is not content with just any food but finds the best, even if she has to travel to purchase it.

❧ Proverbs 31:15 —She rises also while it is still night, and gives food to her household, and portions to her maidens.

Portions are the instructions for the day — portions of work. She has a sense of leadership, so she rises early and sets the example.

❧ Proverbs 31:16 —She considers a field and buys it; from her earnings she plants a vineyard.

She is an entrepreneur. We have seen that she is a woman of valor, but how else does Ruth compare to our Proverbs 31 working woman?

Ruth returned to Bethlehem and went to work as a gleaner in the fields. This was not glamorous work. It was back-breaking! Gleaners bent down to pick up the small grains, which according to Mosaic law, were to be left at the corners of the field for the poor. Ruth was a day worker with no rights and no insurance of protection. However, her job did not determine her attitude. She humbled herself to do what was necessary to gather food and to minister to Naomi.

Since we can read the end of Ruth's book, we know that God not only gave Ruth and her mother-in-law a kinsman redeemer, He also chose her to be in the line of Messiah Himself.

> Matthew 1:5-6 – And to Salmon was born Boaz by Rahab; and to Boaz was born Obed by Ruth; and to Obed, Jesse; and to Jesse was born David the king. And to David was born Solomon by her who had been the wife of Uriah (Bathsheba).

God was aware of Ruth's circumstances and blessed her and enabled her to make significant changes in her life. As we seek to serve the Lord and to be "workers at home," let's remember not only our *Proverbs 31* woman, but also Ruth. Understanding poverty first-hand, Ruth understood the need to minister mercy to those less fortunate. The *Proverbs 31* woman does as well.

- Proverbs 31:20-21 –She extends her hand to the poor; and she stretches out her hands to the needy. She is not afraid of the snow for her household, for all her household are clothed with scarlet.

She is prepared for the colder weather and has even dyed the clothing to give it more beauty; she wants her family to look good.

- Proverbs 31:22 –She makes coverings for herself; her clothing is fine linen and purple.

She dresses to make herself more attractive for her husband and family.

- Proverbs 31:23 –Her husband is known in the gates, when he sits among the elders of the land.

Her husband has the respect of his community; this would indicate that she gives her husband respect and honor at home. Be careful to guard the reputation of your husband and not to gossip about him.

- Proverbs 31:24 —She makes linen garments and sells them, and supplies belts to the tradesmen.

She is industrious and helps with the economic conditions of her family.

- Proverbs 31:25 —Strength and dignity are her clothing, and she smiles at the future.

Her beauty is more than outward. This woman of valor clothes herself in the strength and majesty of the Lord Himself.

ARE YOU DRESSED FOR SUCCESS?

Where does this woman get her dignity or majesty? She knows that her clothing comes from the Lord. Psalm 29:11 says, "The LORD will give strength to His people; The LORD will bless His people with peace." We should also note the following verses:

Psalm 93:1—The LORD reigns, He is clothed with majesty; the LORD has clothed and girded Himself with strength; indeed, the world is firmly established, it will not be moved.

Psalm 104:1—Bless the LORD, O my soul! O LORD my God, Thou art very great; Thou art clothed with splendor and majesty.

Job 40:10—Adorn yourself with eminence and dignity; and clothe yourself with honor and majesty.

How does the New Covenant teach us to clothe ourselves? It says in Ephesians 4:24, "Put on the new self, which in the likeness of God has been created in righteousness and holiness of the truth." We are "to put on" or "be clothed with" (in the sense of sinking into a garment) this new self. Ephesians 6:11 says that we are to "Put on the full armor of God, that you may be able to stand firm against the schemes of the devil."

❧ Proverbs 31:25—And she smiles at the future.

She is not just a positive thinker; rather this phrase is linked to the first phrase, "strength and dignity are her clothing." She does not serve her family in her own puny strength: she is the servant of the Most High God and therefore has access to all of His resources. Her service is a direct result of depending on the clothing of strength and dignity from the Lord.

❧ Proverbs 31:26 –She opens her mouth in wisdom, and the teaching of kindness is on her tongue.

She is a good teacher because she depends on the Master Teacher and His Word. Her actions within the household were determined by God's Word.

❧ Proverbs 31:27—She looks well to the ways of her household, and does not eat the bread of idleness.

Because her family is her main priority, she can manage her household and devote her physical, emotional, and mental strength to building up its members.

❧ Proverbs 31:28 –Her children rise up and bless her; her husband also, and he praises her.

She finds favor and approval from her children and her husband.

> 🐚 Proverbs 31:29 –Many daughters have done nobly, but you excel them all.

Nobly is the same word that is translated as "excellent" or "valor" in Proverbs 31:10.

> 🐚 Proverbs 31:30 –Charm is deceitful and beauty is vain, but a woman who fears the LORD, she shall be praised.

When we praise the Lord, we remind those who love us that our faith does not rest on our own beauty but in the fear of the Lord.

> 🐚 Proverbs 31:31—Give her the product of her hands, and let her works praise her in the gates.

The word "product" is the Hebrew word for fruit, and the only way to bear fruit is to abide in the Messiah and be yielded to the Holy Spirit. John 15:5 says, "I am the vine, you are the branches; he who abides in Me, and I in him, he bears much fruit; for apart from Me you can do nothing."

HAVING YOUR PRIORITIES STRAIGHT

The woman of *Proverbs 31* is valiant, noble, and a woman of excellence because she has her priorities straight. Her reverence and fear of the Lord is the source of wisdom for all that she does. She does not work for her family or even herself but for the Lord Himself.

As she lives to please the Lord, she focuses her life on the true priorities of the woman of God.

This woman, who is the ultimate "worker at home," does not depend on her own strength. God has called you to be a woman of nobility, to be clothed in His dignity and strength.

We can praise the Lord with the psalmist and say, "But Thou, O LORD, art a shield about me, my glory, and the One who lifts my head" (Psalm 3:3).

When you get up each morning, be sure to dress for success as it says in Job 40:10, "Adorn yourself with eminence and dignity; and clothe yourself with honor and majesty." Put your attitude under the control of the Holy Spirit of God, "Whatever you do, do your work heartily, as for the Lord rather than for men; knowing that from the Lord you will receive the reward of the inheritance. It is the Lord Messiah whom you serve" (Colossians 3:23-24).

Recognize your high calling as a woman: as a wife, as a mother, and as a daughter of the King. In the next chapter we will learn about Lydia, a single mother, who was greatly used by the Lord for such a time as this.

THOUGHT QUESTIONS AND REFLECTIONS

1. Think of your attitude as you go about your activities at home. Are you building your home up or tearing it down?

2. What particular qualities of the Proverbs 31 woman speak to your heart?

3. Do you personally see the value in being a worker at home?

4. Consider Proverbs 31:10-31 as a manual for a mother discipling her son in regards to what kind of woman to marry.

5. Consider how you can teach your daughter or a younger woman to pursue being a woman of excellence.

6. Is there a "Naomi" in your life that you could encourage like Ruth did?

7. Do you take your daily responsibilities in the home seriously?

A Virtuous Woman makes linen garments and sells them, and supplies belts to the tradesmen.

Proverbs 31:24

Chapter 9

LYDIA

FOR SUCH A TIME AS THIS

How could a single mother be used of God to start the spread of the Good News into Europe? Before we look at that, let's think a little more about what it means to be an effective "worker at home."

For me, one of the most encouraging aspects of the phrase "workers at home" is that Messiah used the same word for work to describe his own ministry. In the previous chapter, we looked at what Yeshua said to His disciples just after he spoke to the Samaritan woman. Thinking that He must be hungry, Messiah's disciples had wanted Him to eat some food:

John 4:32-34—But He said to them, "I have food to eat that you do not know about." The disciples therefore were saying to one another, "No one brought Him anything to eat, did he?" Messiah said, "My food is to do the will of Him who sent Me, and to accomplish His *work*."

He was telling them that the true sustenance and fulfillment for His life did not come from physical food or physical comforts but from carrying out the will of His Father. This speaks volumes to me. I love to eat -(especially dessert). I thought it was terrific when chocolate - especially dark chocolate - was deemed good for us...practically a health food! But as we all know, the pleasure of physical food is temporary and not all that satisfying. When Sam and I eat out, we know that as unique or interesting as the meal might seem to be at the time, it will soon be forgotten. Unless we have had the opportunity to share the Lord with either the waitress or our dinner guests, the meal becomes an easily forgotten occasion rather then something of eternal value.

An Illusion Or Reality?

There is no more thrilling satisfaction than to know that I am doing what God wants me to do - in my home and marriage, in my ministry, in my friendships, and in my congregation.

When I tried to set my own agenda and fill my life with the things that I wanted, I soon realized that the things that I had thought would fulfill my desires were like mirages in the desert. You have probably seen a movie in which someone who is lost in the desert is desperately searching for water and suddenly sees what appears to be an oasis with a pool of water. But it turns out to be a mirage — an optical phenomenon that creates the illusion of water. It is a distortion of light caused by alternate layers of hot and cold.

From a distance, the illusion looks real, but in reality there is no water - just more sand and empty cisterns.

When both of our sons were young and we lived in a small apartment in the New York area, I used to dream of having a house of our own, thinking that living in a house would make me happier. After visiting friends who lived in nice homes, I would fight envy and discontentment when we went back to our small apartment. But as I matured in the Lord, I discovered that looking to a bigger apartment, a house, a career, or anything but Messiah's sufficient grace (to give me security and happiness) was really like pursuing a mirage in the desert.

Unique By Design

In our secular society, the prevailing perception is that being a homemaker and caring for children demeans a woman's dignity and limits her potential. Perhaps some of us have been swayed by society and think that there must be another way. How could we possibly find contentment and fulfillment in this idea of being a "worker at home"?

When my husband Sam was teaching the book of Jonah, he would often ask, "How many of you would like to know the will of God for your lives?" Invariably, most of the hands in the congregation would go up. Then Sam would respond, "It doesn't always help to know. As Jonah found out, knowing God's will does not necessarily mean that you will want to follow His will." God had given His prophet Jonah His direct will and plan, but Jonah not only refused, he fled in the opposite direction.

Will we follow His will for us to be "workers at home"? Think about it! God created us women in a unique way. Our Designer gave us the privilege of giving birth.

Faithfulness Yields Fulfillment

For our consideration, let's look at a verse that is sometimes difficult to understand.

> 1 Timothy 2:15—But women shall be *saved* through the bearing of children if they continue in faith and love and sanctity with self-restraint.

We know that we are saved by trusting in the atonement of Messiah, so what does it mean that women will be "saved through the bearing of children?"

Salvation in this context means even more than escape from eternal judgment. It comes from the Hebrew *yasha* which means to be delivered, to be liberated, be saved, and to give victory.

> Psalm 119:117—Uphold me that I may be *safe*, that I may have regard for Thy statutes continually.

In the New Covenant, the Greek word, *sozo*, means to save, to be safe, and to be *well*. It is used in Luke 8:48, "your faith has made you well."

Peace with God implies not only deliverance from judgment but also fullness of life. Salvation brings wholeness of life. Romans 5:10 says, "For if while we were enemies we were reconciled to God by the death of his Son, much more, now that we are reconciled, shall we be *saved* by his life."

In this verse the same word "saved" is translated to mean both being saved and finding a complete life in God.

For women, the fullness of life that God gives includes our unique gift of child bearing, which leads to discipleship of the next generation. In 1 Timothy 4:16 it refers to a new, fulfilling life and relationship with God:

> 1 Timothy 4:16—Pay close attention to yourself and to your teaching; persevere in these things; for as you do this you will insure *salvation* both for yourself and for those who hear you.

In the phrase "bear children" found in 1 Timothy 2:15, the word bear literally means to rear or parent children. The word can refer not only to raising the children from our own wombs but also to discipling spiritual children. As we see in 2 Corinthians, Paul saw himself as a spiritual parent:

> 2 Corinthians 12:14—Here for this third time I am ready to come to you, and I will not be a burden to you; for I do not seek what is yours, but you; for children are not responsible to save up for their parents, but parents for their children.

Making Disciples

Women should always be disciplers. When we are young we disciple our small children physically and spiritually. When we are older, we follow the instruction given in Titus 2:3-5 to continue to disciple, the older women discipling the younger. A major part of the concept of being "workers at home" is discipling children. This can be a life-long commitment, because spiritual discipleship is always needed.

In 1 Timothy 2:15, "if they continue in faith and love and sanctity with self-restraint" promises that our lives will be fulfilled if we are faithful to our calling from God.

A lifestyle of faithfulness yields a lifetime of fulfillment. Paul calls us not only to find our fulfillment in the rearing or discipling of children but also to develop a lifestyle of faith in God.

We need to acknowledge our dependence on His grace if we want to keep growing in love. God's *agape* love that can be shed abroad in our hearts gives us concern and commitment to the eternal welfare of others as we grow in holiness.

We must "continue in faith and love and sanctity with self-restraint." The word "self-restraint" also means sensibility and has the same root as the Greek word *sofron* that is found throughout Titus 2.

Does this mean that a wife and mother cannot have a job outside the home? No, but it does mean that she should not place her job above her faith, her marriage or her children. Needing to work in order to feed your family is a different scenario from that of working for your own self-esteem, for a larger mansion, or a second vacation.

A woman of valor is *fulfilled* (saved) by raising children as she trusts in God's love to motivate her, His holiness to keep her, and His perspective on who she is in Him. She is to influence humanity from the bottom up, not the top down. Fulfillment comes from fulfilling God's calling by grace alone for His glory.

Lydia ~ A Woman Of Influence

Let's look now at Lydia, the woman who was greatly used by the Lord to influence not only her own household but the entire continent of Europe. We could call Lydia a single-minded, single mother for Messiah.

> Acts 16:13-15, 40—And on the Sabbath day we went outside the gate to a riverside, where we were supposing that there would be a place of prayer; and we sat down and began speaking to the women who had assembled. And a certain woman named Lydia, from the city of Thyatira, a seller of purple fabrics, a worshiper of God, was listening; and the Lord opened her heart to respond to the things spoken by Paul. And when she and her household had been immersed, she urged us, saying, "If you have judged me to be faithful to the Lord, come into my house and stay." And she prevailed upon us. And they went out of the prison and entered the house of Lydia, and when they saw the brethren, they encouraged them and departed.

Even though Paul was an apostle to the Gentiles, he always went to the Jewish community first as he began his ministry in different locations. Philippi was no exception. Paul and his companions spent their first few days exploring the area and developing a plan for reaching out with the Good News. As was his custom, when *Shabbat* came, Paul and his friends sought out the Jewish community.

According to Jewish law, a congregation was made up of ten men called a *minyan*. Wherever there were ten male heads of households who could be in regular attendance, a synagogue was to be formed.

Philippi apparently did not have the *minyan*, or ten men, and so was without a synagogue.

On the *Shabbat*, therefore, Paul and his companions walked outside the city in search of a Jewish place of prayer, probably heading toward the Gangites River about a mile and a half west of the city. There they found some women gathered to recite the Hebrew prayers, to read from the Scriptures (*Tenach*), to discuss what they had read, and, if possible, to hear from a traveling Jewish teacher and receive a blessing. Paul and his companions sat down with these women and began to speak to them.

Here was the apostle who had turned Asia upside down for Messiah and who had been brought by a vision to Philippi, Macedonia in order to open up Europe for the Good News. Some might think, "What a small and inauspicious beginning - preaching to just a few women by a riverside." In fact, Paul's first witness was to a single mom! Scripture teaches us that this single mother became one of Paul's strongest allies and helpers in his ministry. Paul's greatest work in Europe began with Lydia, and we should never "despise the day of small things" (Zechariah 4:10).

If God used a fearful Gideon and his small band of men to defeat the powerful Midianite army, a teenage David to defeat the Philistine giant, Goliath, and Lydia to help reach a continent, then God can use you. Fruitfulness does not depend on your power or strength; it is all about trusting in the power and strength of God.

If you feel like a failure and say in your heart, "I can't do this" then you will ultimately fail. However, if you trust in God's power, His power is made perfect through your weakness. God plans to do a great work through you as you yield your life and your home to Him.

The Lydian Lady

Acts 16:14— A woman named Lydia, from the city of Thyatira, a seller of purple fabrics, a worshiper of God, was listening; and the Lord opened her heart to respond to the things spoken by Paul.

Lydia (or, "the Lydian lady"), was born in Lydia, a Macedonian colony. She was a businesswoman from Thyatira, a place famous for making purple dyes that were in great demand because they were used for the official toga in Rome and in Roman colonies. Lydia must have been a woman of some means to carry on such an important enterprise from her native city. She was also a single mom with a "household" to care for.

Even though she was an industrious business woman, (like the woman in Proverbs 31), she had her priorities straight. In other words, she was a hard worker, which is not a workaholic by definition. On Shabbat, she went to services with her entire household. She prioritized her time so as to honor the Lord. She knew that she and her family needed more than material things. They all needed the Lord.

Do you suppose that as Lydia got her household ready to go to the riverside for prayer and worship that she was praying, "Lord, I desire to know you in a deeper way, please send Your messenger to teach me today?" Perhaps this was the persistent prayer of her heart.

Through Paul, God found Lydia and met her deepest needs because her heart was open and she was seeking God. If you prioritize the Lord and your spiritual needs above all else, then God will meet all your other needs as well. The Scriptures teach, "Seek ye first the kingdom of God, and his righteousness; and all these things shall be added unto you" (Matthew 6:33). Someone asked Emily Post, "What is the correct procedure when one is invited to the White House and has a previous engagement?" She answered, "An invitation to dine at the White House is a command, and automatically cancels any other engagement." An invitation from heaven to come worship the Lord is even greater . For the believer, Messiah claims priority over everything.

A WORSHIPER OF GOD

Lydia was a worshiper of God (Acts 16:14). This phrase "A worshiper of God" was applied to Gentiles who had accepted the Torah's teaching in one God and attended the synagogue but had not become a Jewish proselyte. The Jewish community in Thyatira was especially interested in the dyeing industry, and Lydia in all probability became interested in the God of Abraham, Isaac, and Jacob there.

The word worshiper denotes both worship and reverence for God. Therefore, Lydia was not just impressed by the God of Israel - she worshipped Him.

How is her reverent attitude toward God evidenced? Lydia had a listening ear. A worshiper is a listener. "Heard us" is in the Greek imperfect active form, which denotes that Lydia was listening - really listening - and she kept it up, listening with a hungry heart.

Sometimes I talk too much, especially when I am nervous. It is much better if I can be still before the Lord and let Him speak to me.

As a worshiper of God, her heart was opened. Call it God's open-heart, spiritual surgery. God is the One who opens the heart, but we are the ones who prepare our hearts by listening. Are you open and yielded to what the Lord has for you, or do you first have to decide if it fits into your agenda? When you show faith by listening, God gives grace by opening.

Lydia kept her mind centered on the things spoken by Paul, whose words gripped her attention. She heard, believed, and heeded the teachings. The Lord opens the heart that we might cling to the truth. What is the use of learning if we disregard the information as soon as the message is over?

A doctor has an uncooperative patient. The physician outlines a detailed program of treatment: medicines to take and the proper dose, permitted foods, graduated exercises, and even the right kind of bath.

But all that labor is wasted if the doctor's patient merrily goes on eating what he pleases and taking his medicines when and if he remembers. Likewise, if you are unwilling to trust and follow God, why should He open your heart to His truth?

Lydia had an obedient faith

Lydia believed and was ready to make a public declaration of her faith in Yeshua. Water immersion allowed her to demonstrate her faith. Her household included the residents of her house, who like her, had heard the preaching of Paul and believed. In obedience to Him, those who believe are immersed as a testimony to others.

After Lydia's immersion she urged them to stay. Lydia not only invited them but made an appeal, "And when she and her household had been immersed, she urged us, saying, 'If you have judged me to be faithful to the Lord, come into my house and stay.' And she prevailed upon us." (Acts 16:15)

When the Scriptures say that Lydia "prevailed upon them" she was not just being polite but was demonstrating her sincerity as she pressed them to come. Actually the word has a strong urging as in forcing against nature.

First she reasoned with them to stay at her home. Lydia had confessed her faith and submitted to immersion as proof that she was "faithful to the Lord." If she was fit for that, surely she was fit to be their hostess.

Lydia was a force to be reckoned with. This single mom was strong-minded. We need to be persistent in doing good. When we lived in New York, Sam received a call from a Jewish believer in Connecticut who asked him to start a congregation there.

Sam was already planting one congregation and supervising several others who were planters, and he barely had enough time for all he was doing. However, Ben prevailed upon him to start a congregation in Connecticut, and so Sam and another leader went once a week until a group was formed. The congregation is still going strong to this day! A faithful witness uses the resources that the Lord supplies.

You may say, "I can't preach like Paul, but I have a house that Paul can use for preaching." Soon, it seems, Lydia's home became the center for outreach and worship in Philippi.

She was willing to believe and identify with Messiah through immersion, which meant that she identified publicly with other believers in the community! When we use our time, talent, and treasures for His Good News, we are a witness in the community. Lydia used her home. We can use our time and abilities.

This is how a great work for God is established, not only by a Paul, but also by mothers, ordinary people willing to live forthrightly for the Lord!

Eventually, the little congregation became a key to Paul's ministry in Europe (Philippians 2:25-30; 4:10-19). Like Lydia, you can yield your life to Yeshua. God can do a great work in you, your family, and community.

Thought Questions

1. What are the characteristics of Lydia that you would aspire to?

2. How are you using your time, talent, and treasure?

3. Can you think of a single mother you could encourage to live for the Lord despite her circumstances?

4. Are you listening? Are you worshiping? Are you serving? Then let's live for Messiah!

A Woman of Excellence extends her hand to the poor, and she stretches out her hands to the needy.

Proverbs 31:20

Chapter 10

TABITHA

A LIFE MARKED BY KINDNESS

*Older women ... may encourage the young
women to be ...kind.*
(Titus 2:3-5)

The fifth quality of our study is to be "good" or "kind." In this chapter, I will use these words interchangeably. As I reflected on what it means to be kind, the bumper sticker that reads "Doing Random Acts of Kindness" came to my mind.

I searched for 'Random Acts of Kindness' on the Internet and discovered a myriad of sites, including a research foundation, a camp and a curriculum for classrooms, to name a few. It seems that in our secular, selfish world, doing random acts of kindness is being promoted as a way to get people to do good to one another. But these acts of kindness actually seemed selfish to me, because they are intended to make the doer of the kindness feel good.

For example, if I was walking down a city street and saw that a parking meter had expired, and I knew that a policeman was giving out tickets on that block, I could drop some change in the meter to help that unknown person avoid a fine. I could feel good about myself for being so magnanimous as to drop in a few quarters. Even though it would be a 'random act of kindness,' there would be no need to form a relationship or to follow up in any way. The act might make me feel good about myself, but that means that its end result would be self centeredness.

Random Acts Of Kindness Redefined

These random acts of kindness could be the world's attempt to encourage us to be kind or good. However, an article entitled *We wouldn't advocate random acts of spending. So why treat kindness any less seriously?* by Emuna Braverman made sense to me, because it reflected Biblical values. An excerpt of the article will provide a beneficial backdrop for our study of good.

"Practice Random Acts of Kindness" reads the bumper sticker. Sounds so good, so warm and cozy. But is it the right attitude? Now what kind of Scrooge would find fault with this philosophy? Well, traditional Judaism, for one, would.... Our sages teach us that the world stands on three things: on Torah, on service of God, and on acts of loving kindness (Ethics of Our Fathers, 1:2). Judaism is definitely in favor of kindness! The problem lies in the random nature the bumper sticker alludes to. Why should our acts of compassion and caring be any more random than the other actions in our life?

We wouldn't advocate random acts of spending (except perhaps at a Barney's sale!), or bring that quality of whimsy and serendipity to our workplace. So why treat kindness any less seriously? The Torah teaches that kindness should be offered in a thoughtful and appropriate way. A trivial example may lie in gift giving. Are you taking into account the wishes of the recipient and what gives him or her pleasure; or is it all about you? This is what I would want. Isn't it nice of me to think of them? An act of kindness is a precious gift -- with potential to change a life. But only when it's carefully thought out with the particular needs and sensitivities of the beneficiary in mind; not when it's random. I'm designing a new bumper sticker: "Practice Strategically Planned and Well-Considered Acts of Kindness." Not so catchy, but ultimately more effective. Anybody want one? (Aish.com website)

I think Emuna Braverman gives us a sense of what we older women are to teach younger women. I like her new bumper sticker, because it captures the values that we find in the Scriptures.

When we studied being a "worker at home" we saw that it has nothing to do with mundane household matters but rather with the atmosphere of our home, as we seek to glorify the Lord in all we do. Teaching women to be good or kind gives us a practical strategy for building up our lives, our homes, and our communities.

Reflecting His Goodness

Before we look at the Greek word for "good", let's look at the Hebrew word, which is *tov*. The word *tov* is used at least 290 times in the Hebrew Scriptures.

Psalm 136:1—Give thanks to the LORD, for He is *good*; for His lovingkindness is everlasting.

This commonly used word *tov* has a variety of meanings. The most frequently used are: good, pleasant, agreeable, excellent (of its kind), rich, valuable in estimation, appropriate, becoming.

Psalm 136:1 tells us to give thanks to the Lord. The word for "give thanks," or *hodu* in Hebrew, is in the command form. God commands us to give thanks. But according to this verse, to whom do we give thanks? Of course, we give thanks to the Lord. The verse goes on to tell us why we should give thanks: because He is good. The end of the verse gives us a definition of God's goodness. It says that His lovingkindness, His *Chesed* is forever.

As we seek to be good and to do good, we reflect the character of God Himself, working in us and through us in the power of Holy Spirit. This goodness that reflects His loving kindness is eternal. What does this eternality mean for you and me? If we depend on His power for our goodness, our kindness, and our good deeds, then we will not grow weary in well doing because we will have an eternal supply.

What if the verse had used the opposite of good? Give thanks to the LORD because He is bad, evil, disagreeable, and argumentative. The notion is ludicrous, because it would go against the very nature of God. All of these opposite qualities of good are things that tear down and destroy, which is unlike the Creator God.

We can evaluate the goodness of our deeds by asking if they reflect God's character and His goodness, or if they tear down and destroy.

Doer Of Good Works

Proverbs 22:1 says: "A good name is to be more desired than great riches, favor is better than silver and gold."

In Acts chapter 9, we meet a woman who had a good name because she was a doer of good works. The account of Tabitha, whose name means "gazelle" in Hebrew and is Dorcas in Greek, is recorded in Acts 9:36-42. The passage gives us a snapshot of a woman who was characterized by her good (*agathos*) deeds (*ergon*). The word used for her deeds or work is the same Greek work - *ergon* - that is used in the compound word for workers at home. The word used for "good" is *agathos*, which can also be translated kindness or charity.

We read in Acts 9:36, "Now in Joppa (near modern Tel Aviv) there was a certain disciple named Tabitha (which translated in Greek is called Dorcas); this woman was abounding (full) with deeds of kindness and charity, which she continually did."

We can learn much from this single verse. First of all, Tabitha was a disciple, a follower of the Messiah of Israel and His teachings. Her witness into the community was having a huge impact as she cared for the widows. Widows were members of the community who had limited resources, so they could not pay back her kindnesses.

The end of verse 36 says that Tabitha was abounding with deeds of kindness or, as the New King James version says, she was "full of these good works." Tabitha's life was characterized by ministering to those around her with her whole heart. I believe that she was able to accomplish all these good works because she received kindness and goodness from the Lord as His child. As Messiah's follower, she in turn served those around her by letting His kindness and goodness flow through her.

> Acts 9:37-38 – And it came about at that time that she fell sick and died; and when they had washed her body, they laid it in an upper room. And since Lydda was near Joppa, the disciples, having heard that Peter was there, sent two men to him, entreating him, "Do not delay to come to us."

A Grief Observed

In verse 37, we learn that Tabitha died. It became an urgent matter for the believers, because according to Jewish custom, a body was permitted to remain unburied no longer than three days and three nights. Tabitha's sudden death and the loss of her were more than the widows could bear. As the congregations were in their infancy stage and struggling to be a light in the darkness, Tabitha's influence must have been significant. Notice that even though her ministry was primarily to the widows, a delegation of two men went to talk to Peter to discuss the situation.

These men had to go to the town of Lydda, which was about twelve miles from Joppa. Why did they send two men? According to Jewish law, you need at least two people to give a testimony. For example, a court case required two witnesses testifying in agreement. This is one of the reasons why the Messiah sent out His disciples two by two.

The believers in Joppa chose two men who were able to communicate the urgency of the situation to Peter. When it says the men *entreated* Peter, (verse 38) the word that is used means to exhort, to encourage. The same word is used in 2 Corinthians 5:20, "Therefore, we are ambassadors for Messiah, as though God were *entreating* through us; we beg you on behalf of Messiah, be reconciled to God".

Tabitha, Arise!

Acts 9:39-42 – And Peter arose and went with them. And when he had come, they brought him into the upper room; and all the widows stood beside him weeping, and showing all the tunics and garments that Dorcas used to make while she was with them. But Peter sent them all out and knelt down and prayed, and turning to the body, he said, "Tabitha, arise." And she opened her eyes, and when she saw Peter, she sat up. And he gave her his hand and raised her up; and calling the saints and widows, he presented her alive. And it became known all over Joppa, and many believed in the Lord.

Peter responded positively to these messengers and returned to Joppa. I am sure that during the twelve mile journey he prayed about how to handle this crisis, asking the Lord how he could most effectively minister in the situation.

He must have remembered the time when he had been with Yeshua when He had raised Jarius's daughter from the dead. (Luke 8:49-56) Peter was an eyewitness to the resurrection power of Yeshua, His Lord.

Peter followed Yeshua's example by sending everyone out of the room and praying for this woman as Messiah had prayed for the little girl. Peter commanded Tabitha to wake up and rise. The Lord answered Peter's prayer, and Tabitha came back to life, ready to serve again.

The result of this miracle was not only a great encouragement for the believers in Joppa, but also a witness that caused many to believe and accept the resurrected Yeshua.

As we seek to understand this quality of goodness or doing good deeds, let me ask you a question. Why do you think Tabitha was so loved by the widows? Were they concerned about having the latest fashions?

A Living Example Of Kindness

Good or kind is used to describe her work, and that should be a clue as to how we are to work as well. Tabitha reflected God as her source of goodness in all that she did. Those who had been blessed by her were upset that she was gone because she had displayed God's goodness. That is, she had personalized the character of God to them through her kind deeds. What a witness for His glory! When Peter saw how much she meant to those widows, he prayed that God would raise her from the dead.

In the infant stage of the new congregations, Tabitha was needed as a living example of goodness and kindness. That's what God wants for you and me. We are His ambassadors, His representatives here on earth. God wants to work through you to touch lives in your home, your congregation, and your community. But your greatest impact will not come from the good deeds that you do in your own strength. If you depend on your own flesh, your strength will surely run out. Besides, it is not the deed itself that glorifies God but the attitude behind it.

Be encouraged. Psalm 136:1 says that the lovingkindness that flows from God's character is without end. God's goodness is everlasting, so when He is your resource, you have an unlimited supply. It should give us confidence to understand that God has created us to have an abundance of every good deed. The following verses teach us about the quantity and the quality of our works. He tells the Corinthians to do lots of good deeds and to do them with a cheerful heart.

> 2 Corinthians 9:6-8 –Now this I say, he who sows sparingly shall also reap sparingly; and he who sows bountifully shall also reap bountifully. Let each one do just as he has purposed in his heart; not grudgingly or under compulsion; for God loves a cheerful giver. And God is able to make all grace abound to you, that always having all sufficiency in everything, you may have abundance for every *good* deed.

We are promised quantity and quality for our work. God will give us the grace we need to do every good work He has called us to do. What a promise!

We find another promise in Hebrews 13:20-21. This one reminds us that Jehovah Shalom is the one who enables us to live for Him and to do His will.

Hebrews 13:20-21 —Now the God of peace, who brought up from the dead the great Shepherd of the sheep through the blood of the eternal covenant, even Yeshua our Lord, equip you in every *good* thing to do His will, working in us that which is pleasing in His sight, through Yeshua the Messiah, to whom be the glory forever and ever. Amen.

We do not have to wonder if God wants us to do *good* works. The Scripture says that we are His workmanship and the purpose of our creation is to do good works, not just random acts of kindness but the works that the Lord has prepared for us in His infinite wisdom.

Ephesians 2:10 —For we are His workmanship, created in Messiah Yeshua for *good* works, which God prepared beforehand, that we should walk in them.

Choosing The Good Part

Another example of a woman who understood how to serve her Lord through good works is Miriam (Mary), the sister of Lazarus. Miriam is mentioned three different times in Scripture, and her physical position is the same each time we meet her. Each time we meet her she is at the feet of the Messiah. This reverent posture reflects her heart attitude.

When Martha asked Yeshua to tell Miriam to help her with the good work of serving the food, Messiah told Martha that Miriam had chosen the *good* (*agathos*) part of service. Her good works flowed from her reverent worship.

Luke 10:39-42 –And she had a sister called Miriam, who moreover was listening to the Lord's word, seated at His feet. But Martha was distracted with all her preparations; and she came up to Him, and said, "Lord, do You not care that my sister has left me to do all the serving alone? Then tell her to help me." But the Lord answered and said to her, "Martha, Martha, you are worried and bothered about so many things; but only a few things are necessary, really only one, for Miriam has chosen the *good* part, which shall not be taken away from her."

John 11:32 –Therefore, when Miriam came where Jesus was, she saw Him, and fell at His feet, saying to Him, "Lord, if You had been here, my brother would not have died."

John 12:3 –Miriam therefore took a pound of very costly perfume of pure nard, and anointed the feet of Yeshua, and wiped His feet with her hair; and the house was filled with the fragrance of the perfume.

Let us follow the example of Miriam, the sister of Lazarus. As we yield our hearts to our Lord, we honor Yeshua through our good works. If we rely on Messiah to produce fruit, then the Holy Spirit will make us fruitful.

Galations 5:22-25 –But the fruit of the Spirit is love, joy, peace, patience, kindness, goodness, faithfulness, gentleness, self-control; against such things there is no law. Now those who belong to Messiah Yeshua have crucified the flesh with its passions and desires. If we live by the Spirit, let us also walk by the Spirit.

THOUGHT QUESTIONS

1. How do you see random acts of kindness?

2. Miriam chose the good part that could not be taken away from her. What part do you choose?

3. Define deeds of goodness or kindness?

4. Are you drawing on God's strength and His goodness to show kindness to others?

5. Is there someone in your congregation who you could compare to Tabitha?

6. Do you aften ask the Lord who you can encourage today by an act of kindness?

7. Do you purpose daily to show acts of kindness to your husband? Children? Friends? Neighbors?

*Her husband is known in the gates,
when he sits among the
elders of the land.*

Proverbs 31:23

Chapter 11

IN MESSIAH'S STEPS

SUBMITTING TO YOUR OWN HUSBAND

When is the last time you were having a cup of coffee with a girlfriend and your conversation went something like this? "So Abby, how are the kids doing?" "How's that submission to your husband progressing along? Have you been respecting his authority and submitting to him this week?"

I do not know about you, but this would not be a typical conversation that I would have. In fact, I find submission is not one of my favorite subjects for discussion.

Now, we have come to the final quality that older women are to be teaching younger women. It is the issue of "being subject to you own husband."

Since submission is such an important principle of the Scriptures, we need to have a biblical basis for practicing submission to authority in general.

My prayer is that we see submission as God's will and the way for us that brings true satisfaction and reward. Whether you are married or not, this study will be helpful for your spiritual growth and will equip you to disciple women.

WHAT IS SUBMISSION?

Before we discuss the definition of submission, we first need to understand what it is not. Submission is not subjugation! It is not simply being quiet or being a doormat. But rather submission is willingly placing one's self under the authority of someone else. As wives, we are called to willingly and voluntarily place ourselves under the authority of our own husbands and not to just any man.

In the Greek, the word "submission" is *hupotasso* and means to place or rank under, to subject, or to obey . In the phrase "being *subject* to your own husband" this Greek word is a verb participle that carries the idea of continually placing yourself in a subordinate position or in subjection to authority.

Five Areas Of Submission

Submission is found throughout our society. If we did not practice it, we would have chaos. I would like us to look briefly at five areas of submission.

CHILDREN SUBMITTING TO THEIR PARENTS

The first area regarding submission is children submitting to their parents. The classic portion of Scripture regarding the fact that children should be subject to their parents is found in Ephesians 6:1-3

Ephesians 6:1-3 —Children, *obey* your parents in
the Lord, for this is right. Honor your father and mother
(which is the first commandment with a promise), that
it may be well with you, and that you may live long on
the earth.

The example of our Messiah practicing submissive
behavior when He was a child is particularly encouraging
to me. In Luke, it says that Messiah put Himself under the
authority of his parents.

Luke 2:51—And He went down with them (*his*
parents), and came to Nazareth; and He continued *in*
subjection to them; and His mother treasured all these
things in her heart.

Messiah, who has all authority, understood how the
authority of the home needed to work. How many homes
are in disarray because the children are not being submissive
to their parents? Are we teaching our children this precept
from the Lord and how to apply it to their immediate lives
as well as to their future children?

CITIZENS SUBMITTING TO THEIR GOVERNMENT

The second area of submission is that of citizens
submitting to their government. In Romans 13:1, it tells
us that every one of us needs to be in submission to the
authorities of the government where we reside.

Romans 13:1—Let every person be in subjection
to the governing authorities. For there is no authority
except from God, and those which exist are established
by God.

1 Peter 2:13 reiterates the point: "Submit yourselves for the Lord's sake to every human institution, whether to a king as the one in authority." Can you imagine if we all decided not to obey the traffic police and just did our own thing? Traffic jams and road rage would abound!

EMPLOYEES SUBMITTING TO EMPLOYERS

Thirdly, we have employees submitting to employers. In your office, if no one listened to the supervisor and everyone did what was right in his own eyes, what kind of work place would that be?

> 1 Peter 2:18-20—Servants, be submissive to your masters with all respect, not only to those who are good and gentle, but also to those who are unreasonable. For this finds favor, if for the sake of conscience toward God a man bears up under sorrows when suffering unjustly. For what credit is there if, when you sin and are harshly treated, you endure it with patience? But if when you do what is right and suffer for it you patiently endure it, this finds favor with God.

MEMBERS TO THEIR ELDERS

Fourthly, we have the congregation layperson in submission to the elders of the congregation.

> Hebrews 13:17—Obey your leaders, and submit to them; for they keep watch over your souls, as those who will give an account. Let them do this with joy and not with grief, for this would be unprofitable for you.

Imagine a congregation where everyone does their own thing, and no one is listening to the congregational elders. What a mess that would be!

Think with me for a moment. What would our society look like if no one was in submission to a higher authority. The very decline that we see in society today is due to the fact that there is a lack of submission. The home, work place, community, and congregation must follow the biblical concept of submission!

This then begs the question, "What is the opposite of submission?" Some ideas come to mind: rebellion, disobedience, anarchy, anti-authoritarianism, pride, arrogance, and a battle zone for control are but a handful of examples.

Can you see what our world would look like without submission? In many ways our society is already exploding with many of these negative qualities as the rebellion of mankind in general is seen. But let us not think that this plague of unsubmissiveness is to be found only in our society. The Bible is full of examples of societies that sought their own way, that did not follow after God.

This lack of submissiveness is a product of sin, and as an end result will prove to be the undoing of men and mankind. So lean not on your own understanding but trust in the Lord that His biblical plan of submissiveness is for our good.

Therefore, if you are breathing, part of a household, living under a government, have a job or are part of a congregation, it is reasonable to think that you are already practicing submission in your life.

WIVES BEING SUBJECT TO THEIR OWN HUSBANDS

Now we come to the fifth area of submission which is "wives being subject to their own husbands." In our homes, how do we live out the calling to glorify the Lord in our marriage as we become one flesh (*basar echad*)? We need to understand God's authority structure as it exists between husband and wife. Note, we are not to be in submission to just any man who comes along, but to our own husband. I have already emphasized that the pronouns were not there to describe the first two qualities—*husband-lovers* and *children-lovers*. But in this phrase, there is a definite pronoun, "your own husband."

> Genesis 2:18—Then the LORD God said, "It is not good for the man to be alone; I will make him a helper suitable for him."

DIVINE ORDER EXEMPLIFIED

How does submission work in the nature of our Triune God? To understand this issue of submission, it is helpful to understand that submission is something that is part of God's very nature which can be described as functional subordination. In other words, if we are followers of Messiah, He is our Leader, our Head.

> 1 Corinthians 11:3–But I want you to understand that Messiah is the head of every man, and the man is the head of a woman, and God is the head of Messiah.

We submit or put ourselves under His authority. Following this idea, the fact remains that in the marriage relationship, the man is the head of the woman.

This does not mean that the man is superior to the woman but for the purpose of functionality, God has set His Divine order for harmony to fulfill His purposes. This Divine order is exemplified in the Triune nature of God. As 1 Corinthians 11:3 points out, "God is the head of Messiah."

Does this mean that the Father is somehow better than the Son? No, the Father and Son are equal. Messiah declares, "I and the Father are one" (John 10:30). Messiah is the exact representation of the Father (Hebrews 1:3). However, intrinsic to the nature of the Triune Godhead is relationship (Father, Son and Holy Spirit). How does this relationship between the Father and Son work? Messiah is functionally subordinate to the Father. His subordinate role is part of who He is in relationship to the Father. He is the eternal Son of God who came to do the eternal will of His Father.

How do we apply this concept of Messiah's example of submission to our lives? If we are being conformed to the image of the Son, (Romans 8:29), then our lives should bring glory to Him as we live out God's purpose and will. Remember, we are studying these qualities so that the Word of God will not be dishonored.

In light of this desire to honor God with our lives, I want to focus on how we can honor the Lord by being submissive to our own husbands.

Are men better than women? Are husbands better than wives? Of course not! God created us all equal in His sight. However, in His plan for marriages the Lord has called wives to be functionally subordinate to their husbands.

In order for a marriage to work, we need to understand this subordination. It is totally voluntary. A sensible wife places herself under the authority of her own husband. Again the husband cannot demand this submission. Submission is not forced subjugation. The wife is called to be submissive to her husband just as the husband is called to love his wife sacrificially. (Ephesians 5:25)

How does the relationship between the husband and wife reflect the relationship of God the Father to God the Son? To build a life together takes a unified spirit, will, and humility. Take notice how Messiah did it. In chapter 2 of Philippians, Paul tells us about the humble attitude of our Messiah that we women should emulate and follow.

> Philippians 2:3-5—Do nothing from selfishness or empty conceit, but with *humility* of mind let each of you regard one another as more important than himself; do not merely look out for your own personal interests, but also for the interests of others. Have this attitude in yourselves which was also in Messiah Yeshua.

Some of you may be thinking, "This isn't fair, why do I have to be the one to submit?" This question is worth considering since we have already seen that submission is a part of life and it is the key to have unity in all areas. Paul tells us in the book of Ephesians that being subject to one another is an outworking of our spiritual lives. In other words, whether you are male or female, we are all to submit to one another.

Making The Most Of Our Time

Ephesians 5:15-17—Therefore be careful how you walk, not as unwise men, but as wise, making the most of your time, because the days are evil. So then do not be foolish, but understand what the will of the Lord is.

In Ephesians 5 Paul tells the congregation at Ephesus that they all have the same amount of time to squander or to use wisely. Paul exhorts us to not be foolish squanderers with our time but to understand our calling in the Lord, to be controlled by the Holy Spirit, and to live out this life as we minister to each other. Paul goes on to say:

Ephesians 5:18-21—And do not get drunk with wine, for that is dissipation, but be filled with the Spirit, speaking to one another in psalms and hymns and spiritual songs, singing and making melody with your heart to the Lord; always giving thanks for all things in the name of our Lord Yeshua the Messiah to God, even the Father. And be subject to one another in the fear of Messiah.

We are to be filled or yielded to the Holy Spirit and not be drunk or under the control of wine. Then Paul gives us suggestions as to how we can minister to each other through praise and thanksgiving for all things. Since I love music and love to sing, reading verse 19 is very inspiring to me. But you may be saying, "I can't carry a tune in a bucket, and if I'm singing, it will throw everyone off!" Indeed, if it were about perfect harmony then we would all need to audition and only those with perfect or absolute pitch would be admitted into the chorus. However, what this verse is telling us to do is to lift up the Lord, His promises, His praise, and His worthiness as an attitude that flows from our hearts.

As we noted, this filling of His Spirit will be seen in our praise, worship, thankfulness, and our submission to each other. In verse 21, it says we should do this in fear or respect for one another. In other words, our lives are to be about one "downsmanship" instead of one "upsmanship." We are to submit to one another as to the Lord. As we submit to each other, we are reflecting the very values of God just as the Son is submissive to the Father to do His will.

Earlier, in Ephesians 5:6, Paul tells the congregation in Ephesus to be careful about the deceivers with their words of vanity. Listen ladies, we have been sold a "bill of goods." The feminist movement and our society in general tells us that we should not submit to our husbands! They say, that it is demeaning, it's degrading, etc…But notice verse 8 as Paul exhorts us to walk as children of light. Don't be lulled into a stupor, get out of your spiritual apathy, and live for the Lord.

In verse 22, we are told to be in submission to our own husband because the husband is the head of his wife just as the Messiah is the Head of the congregation.

> Ephesians 5:22-23—Wives, be subject to your own husbands, as to the Lord. For the husband is the head of the wife, as Messiah also is the head of the congregation, He Himself being the Savior of the body.

A marriage is designed to build a life together. However, someone has to be in charge. If the wife is not yielded to the Holy Spirit but is following after her own flesh and looking to her husband to meet her needs, then she may end up being a constant nag or dripping. Proverbs 21:9 says, "It is better to live in a corner of a roof, than in a house shared with a contentious woman."

WHY IS IT SO DIFFICULT TO SUBMIT?

We need to stop here and go back to Genesis to answer that age old question. Why is it so difficult to submit? My rebellious nature seems to overcome me! Here's another news flash: Your rebellion to your husband and your desire to dominate him is part of the curse! In Genesis 3:16, God is speaking to Eve and explaining to her some of the consequences for their sin.

> Genesis 3:16—To the woman He said, "I will greatly multiply Your pain in childbirth, in pain you shall bring forth children; yet your *desire* shall be for your husband, and he shall rule over you."

The Hebrew word for desire is *teshuqah* and it means a longing, a desire like that of a beast to devour. As soon as the intimacy with God was broken by sin, Eve lost contentment in her role as the helpmate to her husband. Now her deep desire was not one of submission but rather one of dominance over her husband. We find this same word, *desire*, used for the sin that wanted to dominate and devour Cain.

> Genesis 4:7—If you do well, will not your countenance be lifted up? And if you do not do well, sin is crouching at the door; and its *desire* is for you, but you must master it.

God is speaking to Cain who was sulking because the Lord did not accept his grain offering. The idea is that sin's *desire* overtakes or controls Cain as he gives into it.

Sin had become his master. And indeed, sin did master Cain as he let his hurt pride and jealousy move him to murder his brother.

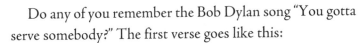

Do any of you remember the Bob Dylan song "You gotta serve somebody?" The first verse goes like this:

> You may be an ambassador to England or France,
> You may like to gamble, you might like to dance,
> You may be the heavyweight champion of the world,
> You may be a socialite with a long string of pearls

Then the chorus:

> But you're gonna have to serve somebody, yes indeed
> You're gonna have to serve somebody,
> Well, it may be the devil or it may be the Lord
> But you're gonna have to serve somebody.

Doesn't his chorus ring true? If you are not submitted to the Lord and serving Him, then you are giving yourself over to your flesh and giving the devil the authority in your life! The question remains. Who are you serving?

BUT, MY HUSBAND DOESN'T FOLLOW THE LORD

Some may be saying, "Listen, I thought my husband was a believer when we got married. We went to services together, and he was able to sing the songs and even find the book of Genesis. But now my husband has no interest in spiritual matters. In fact, I'm not sure if he is a believer. Do I still have to be submissive? Can't I just do my own thing since I'm the one still following the Lord and he isn't?"

Actually, the Scriptures are crystal clear about this point. The fact is, Peter wrote a whole section of his first epistle just for those of us who are married to men who are either unbelievers or carnal believers. Though a woman may be outspoken elsewhere, she is to realize the authority issue in her role as a wife.

Following Yeshua's Example

1 Peter 3:1—*In the same way*, you wives, be submissive to your own husbands so that even if any of them are disobedient to the word, they may be won without a word by the behavior of their wives.

Before we consider these verses from 1 Peter 3, we need to see this verse in context because 1 Peter 3:1 begins with the phrase, "in the same way." What does "in the same way" refer to? In order to understand this phrase, we need to look back at the context in 1 Peter 2:

1 Peter 2:21-25—For you have been called for this purpose, since Messiah also suffered for you, leaving you an example for you to *follow in His steps*, who committed no sin, nor was any deceit found in His mouth; and while being reviled, He did not revile in return; while suffering, He uttered no threats, but kept entrusting Himself to Him who judges righteously; and He Himself bore our sins in His body on the cross, that we might die to sin and live to righteousness; for by His wounds you were healed. For you were continually straying like sheep, but now you have returned to the Shepherd and Guardian of your souls.

This passage follows Peter's teaching on being submissive to those who are treating you in an unreasonable way. Peter tells us that we are called to this specific situation, and if we patiently endure, we will find favor with God. Peter goes on to explain that we are called to follow Messiah's example and imitate His response to suffering.

To help us understand how Messiah bore up under suffering, Peter quotes Isaiah 53:9, where we have the prophetic description of the suffering Lamb of God who committed no sin in word or deed. We learn from Messiah's sinless life how he responded to both verbal accusations and the evil actions against Him. Yeshua exemplifies our enablement in the Lord, which is needed to get us through miserable circumstances.

WHAT WOULD YESHUA DO WHEN BEING REVILED?

1 Peter 2:23 says, "and while being reviled, He did not revile in return." The word "revile" means to employ all kinds of foul reproaches and accusations. Some of you reading this book may have husbands who say nasty things to you or accuse you falsely. The reviling may have to do with verbal abuse where your faith is belittled. Comments such as these could be hurled at you, "You are such an idiot to believe in God. Do you really think He loves you?" These insults can make you think that you are stupid and a loser for trusting in the promises of God.

What did Messiah do when He was reviled? He did not respond in kind but rather gave Himself to His Father who does all things righteously. He entrusted the insults to the One whom He trusted completely. When we are reviled, we can give it to God as well and say with confidence, "I trust You, Lord, in these horrible circumstances; I am depending solely on You, knowing that You will bring me through."

WHAT WOULD YESHUA DO WHEN BEING THREATENED?

The second aspect of Messiah's suffering has to do with evil actions that were perpetrated by His enemies against Him. When He was tormented, He did not retaliate back. Yeshua could have easily said something to those who sought to do Him harm. But what did Messiah do when He was spoken falsely against and was persecuted? "He kept entrusting Himself to His heavenly Father who judges righteously" (1 Peter 2:23).

With Yeshua as our example, we need to respond to those (including our husbands who may accuse or mistreat us) the way He responded to those who accused Him.

Instead of orienting His life around the offender and the offense, Yeshua oriented His life around His Heavenly Father. He entrusted or gave the situation back into His Father's hands. Don't let your husband become the focus of your attention from fear or bitterness. Don't say in your heart, "If I can only hurt him as he has hurt me, then he'll know how it feels when he says those hateful things." Rather, have faith in the Lord and keep entrusting your life into the capable Hands of the One who always does righteously. The Lord will bring His judgment to bear, as needed. He will vindicate you, His servant. As you orient your life around the Lord and His calling for you, He can change your husband's heart. Believe God and entrust your life to Him in the midst of your suffering.

1 Peter 4:19—Therefore, let those also who suffer according to the will of God entrust their souls to a faithful Creator in doing what is right.

You are being watched

With this background we come to 1 Peter 3:1 which as we noted begins with the phrase "in the same way."

> 1 Peter 3:1—In the same way, you wives, be submissive to your own husbands so that even if any of them are disobedient to the word, they may be won without a word by the behavior of their wives.

Peter exhorts us to be submissive to our own husbands. Why? We have already seen that as wives we are called upon to submit or voluntarily place ourselves under the authority of our own husbands. In verse one Peter tells us why. He penned these words under the inspiration of the Holy Spirit. It says that even if your husband is disobedient to the Word or refuses to comply with God's way, he can be won back to the Lord. Being disobedient to the Word can mean one of two things. Either he is saved but living a carnal life, or he is unsaved. In either situation the need is the same. He needs to come back to God and get right with the Lord.

To win him without a word does not mean living in total silence, rather it means responding to your husband by following the example of Messiah. It certainly does not suggest hammering your husband with Scripture verses. If you look to the Lord in the midst of your trials, you will be able to forgive and live in a way that witnesses to Messiah's power at work in you. 1 Peter 3:2 says that our husbands can be won, "as they observe your chaste and respectful behavior." The word *observe* means to watch carefully. We saw the same idea given in 1 Peter 2.

1 Peter 2:12—Keep your behavior excellent among the Gentiles, so that in the thing in which they slander you as evildoers, they may on account of your good deeds, as they *observe* them, glorify God in the day of visitation.

According to this verse, those who criticize us observe the behavior of those who truly follow Yeshua, and their slanderous behavior is proven to be false. Eventually they are forced to acknowledge our goodness and therefore glorify God. This is how it should work for a wife and her husband. An unbelieving husband watches his wife attentively and sees the reality of her faith by her actions, not her words. This lifestyle or behavior is described by two words: chaste and respectful.

We studied the word "chaste" or "pure" (*hagnos*) when we discussed purity. Remember that it means to be free from ceremonial defilement, holy, sacred. As your husband watches your behavior and the way in which you respond to him and to circumstances, if you reflect the Lord, he will be won to Him.

RESPECTING THE POSITION

Respect his position! Your behavior should show respect for the position of your husband even if you think you cannot respect him or his actions. Imagine that you are speeding and a policeman stops you, asking to see your license and registration. Do you look at him and say, "Officer, before I give you my license I need to ask you, have you been kind to your family today? Do you love your wife as Messiah loved the Congregation?" That sounds ludicrous and silly doesn't it?

The policeman has earned his position by virtue of his training and his appointment by the authority of the Highway Patrol. Out of respect for his position, you would submit to his request. In a similar way, God has put your husband in a position of authority over you. If you will respect the position of your husband even when he is being disobedient to God then according to 1 Peter 3, the Lord will bless you.

A few years ago, I taught this study to a group of Jewish believers in the Ukraine. It was the first time that many of them had heard this teaching. One lovely older woman whose husband was unsaved approached me excitedly on the second day of the conference. Through a translator she joyously exclaimed, "It worked! I went home and treated my husband with respect. I did not change what I was doing for him, but my attitude was different as I yielded my life to the Holy Spirit and chose to respect my husband. For the first time he did not ridicule my faith. He was warm and tender to me. Thank you for this teaching, and with the Lord's help I will continue to submit to his authority and honor him while I pray for him to come to know the Lord."

An exceptional situation

There are a few exceptional situations that would require you to disobey your husband. If your husband asks you to break a law, then you must obey God's higher law. When told that they could not share the Gospel in Jerusalem, Peter and the apostles answered to the authorities, "We must obey God rather than men" (Acts 5:29).

If you or your children are in danger or being threatened by your husband, you should leave or get help even call the police.

In general, however, if a wife is submissive to God, she will fulfill her calling as a wife and submit to her husband, regardless of his spiritual condition.

How to win your husband

1 Peter 3:3-4—And let not your adornment be merely external -braiding the hair, and wearing gold jewelry, or putting on dresses; but let it be the hidden person of the heart, with the imperishable quality of a gentle and quiet spirit, which is precious in the sight of God.

Peter gives us further insight into how we can win our husbands "without a word." He is not speaking against braided hair or jewelry or wearing dresses! The problem is not the clothes but the idea of being ostentatious in our dress. Peter is saying not to prioritize the externals to boost your sense of self-esteem. Stop focusing on externals: hairstyles, putting on jewelry, and fine clothes.

Some wives who have a bad relationship with their spouses may emphasize their external appearance to be more alluring or to feel better about themselves. She may want to attract the attention of other men so she will feel desirable or distract herself from her inner pain. However, Peter exhorts wives to work on the inner person rather than on the outer one.

A Spiritual Makeover!

What does God value? Verse four tells us that it is "the imperishable quality of a gentle and quiet spirit." God values most the internal beauty of the soul. We need to work on the "inner heart" as we yield our lives to Him and let Him do a spiritual makeover. Our beauty should be reflecting Messiah's character and glory, which is eternal, imperishable, and more precious than gold. Notice the word imperishable - this beauty does not fade away. Imperishable means that your inner beauty is incorruptible, immortal, and will not decay. We wives do not need a facelift but a heart transformation.

BEAUTIFUL IN HIS SIGHT

Where is this beauty found? It is in the secret, hidden place -that no one except your Creator knows: your soul, your heart, the real you. This eternal, immortal person is worth prioritizing because she is imperishable. God sees the eternal value of your soul as precious and very costly. He does not want it to be influenced by the transitory nature of this life but focused on that which is eternal.

In that way, we can live lives that reflect eternity, and this is precious in God's sight. In 1 Peter 3:5, we are given encouragement from the women of Scriptures who have gone before us.

> 1 Peter 3:5 —**For in** this way in former **times** the holy women also, **who hoped** in God, used **to adorn** themselves, being **submissive** to their own **husbands.**

These women were holy: their lives were consecrated or set apart to God. They also hoped in God, which means that they had confidence in the Lord, trusting in His Word and His promises.

HARMONY IN THE SUBMISSION

According to this verse, these godly women of the past honored God by being submissive to their own husbands. The word "adorn" is *kosmos* which means order or arrangement. These holy women adorned themselves by putting their lives into harmony with God's will by being submissive. As wives, we cannot say that we are relying on God and then rebel to the delegated authority that He has established. If our lives are consecrated to the living God then we will find confidence and hope to live in light of His Word.

We have met several of these holy women throughout this book including Hannah, Lydia, and Abigail. Like them, we want our lives to bring honor and not dishonor to the Lord.

In 1 Peter 3:6, we go from holy women in general to Sarah in particular as Peter explains why God is pleased with her inward response to Abraham.

1 Peter 3:6—Thus Sarah obeyed Abraham, calling him lord, and you have become her children if you do what is right without being frightened by any fear.

Peter is referring to Genesis 18:12 when Sarah is listening by the tent door and hears the outlandish prophecy that she will have a child.

She laughs within herself and asks the question, "After I have become old, shall I have pleasure, my lord being old also?" When the Scripture says that Sarah obeyed Abraham, it means that she put herself under her husband's authority. When did Sarah call him "lord"? Look at the verse. The point is not that she laughed but how she laughed. This was an internal happening. No one except God knew that she had laughed. But she did. She called Abraham, *adoni* or "my lord."

She was acknowledging in her heart that her husband was her master. In 1 Peter 3:6, God promises us that we can become children of Sarah if we do what is good (*agathos*). Her activity reflected God's Word and His character.

The promise for us is that we do not have to be afraid or terrified to follow God's way of doing things.

As we said earlier, men are not superior to women, and the Scriptures do not tell us to submit to every man. According to God's plan, we choose to marry and place ourselves under the authority of the husband whom the Lord brings into our lives.

A Vessel of great value

This is what 1 Peter 3:7 speaks of, "You husbands likewise, live with your wives in an understanding way, as with a weaker vessel, since she is a woman; and grant her honor as a fellow heir of the grace of life, so that your prayers may not be hindered." This does not mean that women are essentially weaker then men.

Many strong, capable women lead corporations or are the leaders of countries. This picture of a weaker vessel is like a ming vase: something very valuable. It says to husbands that their wives have chosen of their own free will to place themselves in a "weaker" position or under the authority of their husbands. Therefore, the husbands are to grant honor to their wives because they are fellow heirs of the grace of life.

Consider who you are in the Lord: you are a subject of the King of Kings and a daughter of the Most High God. As we yield our lives to the Lord and submit to His authority, we are enabled by His grace to live out our calling as wives in the marriage relationship and submit to our own husbands.

Thought Questions

1. Whether you are an older woman or a younger woman, please consider, "Will I live for Him regardless of my circumstances?"

2. How would our society function if no one were in submission to one another?

3. Has God called me to either disciple someone or be discipled myself?

4. Do I look to my husband to meet my needs that only God can fulfill?

5. How will my response to the notion of submission be different if I am controlled by the Holy Spirit, rather than controlled by my flesh?

6. Is your life honoring God?

7. Are you reflecting His values and His character as you live out your life as a woman, a wife, a mother, and a friend?

8. Does He have first place in your life, above yourself, your husband, or your children?

9. Are you trying to find fulfillment apart from God's priorities?

A Woman of Valor who can find?
For her worth is far above jewels.

Proverbs 31:10

Chapter 12

Reflecting His Glory

Concluding Thoughts

Mazel Tov! You are a woman of valor—*eschet hayil*! We have finished our study and my prayer is that you see Yeshua as the source of your fulfillment and the Giver of abundant life! (John 10:10)

We have learned that older women are to teach younger women seven aspects of *Sense and Sensibility*:

- Husband-Lover
- Children- Lover
- Being of Sound Mind
- Purity or Chastity
- Worker at Home
- Goodness or Kindness
- Submission to Your Own Husband

I trust that you will seek to disciple younger women, who need to understand these qualities if they are to mature and honor God with their lives. In Hebrew, seven (*sheva*) is a number that means completion, wholeness, fullness, and perfection. Genesis 2:2 states that God completed His work of creation on the seventh day, and in Genesis 7:2, the number seven is used to describe the complete provision for Noah found in the animals he was to take on the ark.

Seven (*sheva*) is the root word for the Hebrew word "week," *shavua*—a complete or full seven days.

We will find our fullness and completeness in our calling to be women of God as we mature and grow in these seven qualities. In Proverbs 31:10, the question is raised, "Who can find a virtuous woman? For her price is far above rubies" (also translated jewels, corals, pearls). The comparison of a woman to precious jewels indicates the great value of a woman who trusts in God. Taken together, the seven qualities that we have studied are like a beautifully faceted diamond. Admittedly, most of us feel more like diamonds in the rough. However, as we yield our hearts and minds to the Lord, He can smooth out the rough edges and polish us. As He pours out His grace into our lives, we can become brilliant gems for Him.

The beauty of my life will shine into the lives of others as I reflect His glory and honor. As it says in Proverbs 4:18, "The path of the righteous is like the light of dawn, that shines brighter and brighter until the full day." Are you becoming a beautiful, seven faceted diamond who will bring honor to the Lord?

We should be diligent to study this material for ourselves and to teach it to others so "that the word of God may not be dishonored." As we live out these seven qualities, by God's grace and enablement, our lives will indeed bring honor to His name, and His Word will not be dishonored. We are complete in Messiah. Colossians 2:10 says, "And in Him you have been made complete, and He is the head over all rule and authority."

Do you see that God's calling for you to be a woman of God is His eternal purpose for you?

> 2 Corinthians 4:5-7—For we do not preach ourselves but Messiah Yeshua as Lord, and ourselves as your bond-servants for Yeshuas' sake for God, who said, "Light shall shine out of darkness," is the One who has shone in our hearts to give the light of the knowledge of the glory of God in the face of Messiah. But we have this treasure in earthen vessels, that the surpassing greatness of the power may be of God and not from ourselves.

The Lord does not need your talent or skills; He only requires your willingness to yield and obey Him. He will use your "earthen vessel" as you submit to His authority and enablement. When earthen vessels were used in daily life, they did not have to be expensive or sturdy in order to be useful. An earthen vessel is fully functional as long as the light can be seen through it!

God created you as a woman and has called you to serve Him. Yield your heart to Him day by day and let Him accomplish His will through your earthen vessel.

Throughout my thirty-eight years of ministry, one of my favorite verses has been "For I am confident of this very thing, that He who began a good work in you will perfect it until the day of Messiah Yeshua" (Philippians 1:6). Another is 1 Thessalonians 5:24, "**Faithful** is He who calls you, and He also will bring it to **pass.**" Both verses emphasize that God works in me for His purposes, and that He will faithfully complete His will in and through me. Paul points out that we have great reason to hope because God's resurrection power is in us and we have eternity ahead of us. So don't give up!

> 2 Corinthians 4:14-15 –Knowing that He who raised the Lord Yeshua will raise us also with Yeshua and will present us with you. For all things are for your sakes, that the grace which is spreading to more and more people may cause the giving of thanks to abound to the glory of God.

Do you depend on His grace to fill you and flow through you so that many will praise God? 2 Corinthians 4:16 says, "Therefore we do not lose heart, but though our outer man is decaying, yet our inner man is being renewed day by day."

It is always too soon to quit. We are all getting older, and some of us are showing it and feeling it more than others. The great news is that our inner self, the eternal being that will live forever, can be renewed with vigor and sustenance each day. We must not allow ourselves to get weary in our efforts to honor God with our lives.

I pray that He would grant you, according to the riches of His glory, to be strengthened with power through His Spirit in the inner man (Ephesians 3:16).

Each day you need to spend time with the Lord, depending on Him to understand His character and His Word, so that your inner person, your heart, and your mind will be transformed and renewed. Remember that when trials come, our inner lives will be seen for what they are.

2 Corinthians 4:17-18—For momentary, light affliction is producing for us an eternal weight of glory far beyond all comparison, while we look not at the things which are seen, but at the things which are not seen; for the things which are seen are temporal, but the things which are not seen are eternal.

When we hold eternal values, we realize that it is worth everything to bring honor to our Creator. I pray that you have been challenged not only to yield your own life to the Lord, but you will also seek to disciple younger women who desperately need a biblical foundation for their lives. We need to teach women to love and respect the idea of marriage and children, to be in their right minds about themselves, and to live purely so they can minister in their homes. Doing good and voluntarily placing ourselves under the authority of our own husbands will become our regular practice of our lives, and we will bring honor to the name that is above every name: Messiah Yeshua our Lord.

Remember that you are a daughter of the King of Kings and a servant of the Most High God. Let your light shine as a beautiful diamond for Him.

BIBLIOGRAPHY

The works listed below had an influence on my study of Titus 2:3-5 during my preparation of this book.

Alden, Robert L. *Proverbs, A Commentary on an Ancient Book of Timeless Advice*, Baker, 1983

Arthur, Kay, *A Marriage Without Regrets*, Harvest House Publishers, 2000

Bingham, Dottie, *Grace for the Rest of Your Life*, Gracestoration, 1990

Boa Kenneth, *Conformed to His Image*, Zondervan, 2001

Bridges, Charles, *Proverbs A Geneva Series Commentary*, The Banner of Truth Trust, 1977

Crittenden, Danielle, *What Our Mothers Didn't Tell Us*, Simon & Schuster New York, 2000

Cohen, A, *Soncino Books of the Bible, Proverbs*, The Soncino Press 1980

Edersheim, Alfred, *The Life and Times of Jesus the Messiah*, MacDonald Publishing Company

Fructenbaum, Arnold, *The Messianic Jewish Epistles*, Ariel Press, 2005

George, Elizabeth, *A Woman's High Calling*, Harvest House Publishers, 2001

Getz, Gene and Elaine, *The Measure of a Woman*, Regal from Gospel Light, 2004

Heller, Abraham, *The Vocabulary of Jewish Life*, Hebrew Publishing Company, 1942

MacArthur, John, *Different by Design*, Victor Books, 1997

MacArthur, John, *Ruth and Esther: Women of Faith, Bravery and Hope*, Nelson Impact, 2000

Moore, Beth , *A Heart Like His*, Broadman & Holman Publishers, 2003

Nadler, Sam, *Messianic Life Lessons from The Book of Jonah*, Word of Messiah Ministries, 2005

Nadler, Sam, *Messianic Wisdom*, Word of Messiah Ministries, 2003

Morgan, Robert, *Nelson's Book of Stories, Illustrations and Quotes*, Nelson, 2000

Pink, A. W., *The Life of David*, Baker Book House, 1981

Powell, Ivor, *Luke's Thrilling Gospel*, Kregel Publications 1965

Ryle, J.C., *Ryle's Expository Thoughts on the Gospels Volume Two Luke*, Baker, 1977

BOOKS AND MATERIALS BY
WORD OF MESSIAH MINISTRIES

1. **The Feasts of Israel** - Eye-opening! The meaning of Israel's Feasts in light of the New Covenant: *Passover, Firstfruits, Shavuot, Trumpets, Yom Kippur, Sukkot, Hanukkah, Purim* . (232 pp.)

2. **Messianic Life Lessons from the Book of Jonah** - the book of Jonah reveals a Holy, Almighty God who loves people desperately, and will go to any lengths, or depths to reach lost and sinful people. This book will help you to discover God's purpose and plan for your life and rather than flee His will, you may fulfill it! (150pp.)

3. **The Messianic Answer Book** - Answers to the 14 most common questions Jewish people have about The Faith. An excellent tool to share with those seeking 'The Answer'! (112 pp.)

4. **Following Yeshua: Foundational Discipleship for Messianic Believers** - Develop a solid foundation by learning the basic truths needed to grow in God's love. (64 pp.)

5. **Growing in Messiah: Vital Truths for Maturing Messianic Believers** - Answers to challenging questions faced by Jewish and non-Jewish believers in Yeshua. Can be used as a sequel to "Following Yeshua" (123pp.)

6. **Messianic Wisdom: Practical Scriptural Answers for Your Life** - Discover your Jewish roots, get a better grasp on Jewish issues and living out your faith in Messiah. Essential, practical, and inspiring, this book is a must for every growing disciple of Yeshua. (200 pp.)

7. **Even You Can Share The Jewish Messiah!** - Share your faith with Jewish people in a sensitive, effective manner. "Do's and Don'ts", history of 'the Church' and the Jews, prophecy chart. (28 pp.)

8. **The Messianic Passover Haggadah** - The perfect guide for conducting your own Passover Seder, for family or congregational use, or to simply learn more about Messiah and Passover. (40 pp.)

9. **Is Jesus the Messiah? A Study of Isaiah 53** - A four message series with an in-depth look at the Scriptures, history, and ancient rabbinical comments, that proves conclusively that Yeshua truly is the Jewish Messiah. (CDs or Audio cassette)

10. **To The Jew 1st!** - God's priority of taking the Gospel to the Jewish community from Romans 1:16,17; *how* to share with Jewish friends from *The Jewish Evangelism Seminar*. (9 Msgs., CDs / Tapes)

11. **Alive Again! The Resurrection of Messiah** - Investigate the single most provable event in history, on which the entire Messianic Faith stands or falls. From Yeshua's sacrificial death, to His burial, to His empty tomb and ascension, discover what it means for you. (8 msgs.)

12. **Holocaust: A Biblical Response** - A two tape, four message series including 'Yom HaShoah'/Holocaust Remembrance Service, testimony of Holocaust survivor, 'Anti-Semitism is Anti-God', and 'Escape Israel's Future Holocaust' (Zech. 14). Moving, informative, and challenging. (4 msgs., CDs / Tapes)

If you would like to schedule Miriam Nadler to speak at
your next conference or retreat
please contact:

WORD OF MESSIAH MINISTRIES
P.O. BOX 79238
CHARLOTTE, NC
28271, USA

PHONE/FAX: (704) 362-1927

Visit our website at:

WWW.WORDOFMESSIAH.ORG

"Sense & Sensibility"
by Miriam Nadler
Copyright © 2006 Word of Messiah Ministries
Printed in the United States of America
All rights reserved.
ISBN0-9702619-9-3